CROSSINGS

Nietzsche and the Space of Tragedy

JOHN SALLIS

THE UNIVERSITY OF CHICAGO PRESS

Chicago and London

JOHN SALLIS, the W. Alton Jones Professor of Philosophy at
Vanderbilt University, is the author of six previous books including
Spacings—Of Reason and Imagination, published by the University of
Chicago Press.

The University of Chicago Press, Chicago 60637
The University of Chicago Press, Ltd., London
© 1991 by The University of Chicago
All rights reserved. Published 1991
Printed in the United States of America

00 99 98 97 96 95 94 93 92 91   5 4 3 2 1

Library of Congress Cataloging-in-Publication Data
Sallis, John, 1938–
Crossings : Nietzsche and the space of tragedy / John Sallis.
    p.   cm.
Includes bibliographical references and index.
ISBN 0-226-73436-6 (alk. paper). — ISBN 0-226-73437-4 (pbk. :
alk. paper)
    1. Nietzsche, Friedrich Wilhelm, 1844–1990. Geburt der Tragödie.
2. Greek drama (Tragedy)—History and criticism.   3. Tragic, The.
4. Music—Philosophy and aesthetics.   5. Dionysus (Greek deity)
6. Apollo (Greek deity)   7. Deconstruction.   8. Literature—
Philosophy.   9. Metaphysics.   I. Title.
B3313.G43S24   1991
193—dc20   90-43060

Contents

Acknowledgments

Two preparatory studies for this book have appeared as papers: "Apollo's Mimesis," *Journal of the British Society for Phenomenology* 15 (1984); and "Dionysus—In Excess of Metaphysics," in *Exceedingly Nietzsche: Aspects of Contemporary Nietzsche Interpretation,* edited by David Farrell Krell and David Wood (London: Routledge, 1988). I am grateful to the editors for permission to draw upon these papers. I am doubly grateful to David Krell, at whose invitation I presented at the University of Essex a series of lectures that were invaluable in developing the reading given here. I want also to thank Nancy Fedrow, Kristine Sandy, and Jerry Sallis for their generous assistance.

Paris
June 1989

Texts and Abbreviations

Nietzsche

    Werke: Kritische Gesamtausgabe. Ed. Giorgio Colli and
    Mazzino Montinari. Berlin: Walter de Gruyter. All
    texts available in this edition are cited from it by
    volume number and page numbers (without further
    designation).

BKG   *Briefwechsel: Kritische Gesamtausgabe.* Ed. Giorgio Colli
    and Mazzino Montinari. Berlin: Walter de Gruyter,
    1975–.

M   *Gesammelte Werke.* Musarion Edition. Munich: Musarion
    Verlag, 1920–29.

W   *Werke.* Leipzig: Alfred Kröner Verlag, 1912.

WM   *Der Wille zur Macht.* Ed. Peter Gast and Elisabeth
    Förster-Nietzsche. Stuttgart: Alfred Kröner Verlag,
    1959.

Schopenhauer

WWV *Die Welt als Wille und Vorstellung.* Cotta-Verlag/Insel
    Verlag, n.d. Citations are by volume and section
    number.

Wagner

RW   *Werke.* Frankfurt-am-Main: Insel Verlag, 1983.

Greek Tragedies

    References are given in the text by line number.

LB   Aeschylus, *The Libation Bearers*

B   Euripides, *The Bacchae*

E   Euripides, *Electra*

OC   Sophocles, *Oedipus at Colonus*

OT   Sophocles, *Oedipus Tyrannos*

All translations of German texts are my own, though I have consulted available translations, especially Walter Kaufman's translations of Nietzsche. Translations of Greek tragedies are adapted from available translations, especially those collected in *Greek Tragedies,* edited by David Grene and Richmond Lattimore (Chicago: University of Chicago Press, 1960).

Das Masslose

To Peter Gast, postmarked Turin, 4 January 1889:

To my maestro Pietro
Sing me a new song: the world is transfigured
and all the heavens rejoice.

> The Crucified

Afterwards there is only silence.

But scarcely a month before, at the very end of *Ecce Homo,*
Nietzsche had written:.

Have I been understood?—*Dionysus versus* [gegen] *the Crucified* . . . (VI
3: 372)

Thus are posed the two antagonists: almost as if with arms crossed,
prepared to fight for life, Dionysus against the god on the cross.
The ellipsis marks the struggle about to commence.

A few months earlier:

The god on the cross is a curse on life, a sign that one is to redeem oneself
from life;—Dionysus cut to pieces is a *promise* of life: it will be eternally
reborn and return again from destruction. (WM §1052)

Thus speaks the disciple of the philosopher Dionysus: against the
god on the cross, whose crossing brings death to life, crossing out
life with the sign of its curse, with the promise of a life that would
be—death. Dionysus would cross over differently from death to
life, *back* to life, intertwining the opposites, dismembered and yet
eternally reborn.

It cannot have completely escaped Nietzsche—despite all the
gestures of inversion—that Plato, too, wrote of such crossings,
most openly in the story of Er's descent to Hades (identified with
Dionysus by Heraclitus in a fragment that Nietzsche recalls in one
of his notebook entries: "Dionysus is Hades according to Her-

aclitus" [III 3: 82]). The story comes at the end of the *Republic* when Socrates, having driven the poets from the city and seemingly sealed their fate by banishing them to the remote region of mimesis, translates the deeds of the dialogue itself into a story. As that story is coming to an end, Socrates tells how Er was prevented from drinking the water and how therefore the tale (μῦθος) was saved—everything except the tale of Er's rebirth, for Er did not know how he came back into his body. Socrates exhorts Glaucon: if we are persuaded by this tale, we shall make a good crossing (ἐυ δια-βησόμεθα) of the river of Lethe (*Rep.* 621 c).

The contest between philosophy and poetry, in the midst of which Socrates has told of Er's crossing, is recalled and reinstigated by Nietzsche, resumed as a contest between Socrates and the tragic poets. Indeed, this contest provides the frame on which Nietzsche weaves his first story of that comprehensive unfolding that today, after Nietzsche and after Heidegger, one would call the history of metaphysics, even if that frame cannot but call into question the singularity of this history.

In 1888 Nietzsche retells the story of the history of metaphysics. By then it has become a story of the overturning of Platonism. In the century since Nietzsche told "How the 'True World' Finally Became a Fable" (VI 3: 74–75), the story has been so often retold, retelling layered upon retelling, that it can no longer *simply* be told. Let it be said only that the story sets everything adrift: for it is a story of how the ground in which all would be anchored begins to drift away, becoming more and more remote until it remains only something told of in a story, in the story that will just have been told. It is with this story, in telling it, that—as Heidegger retells it—"the overturning of Platonism became for Nietzsche a twisting free of it [*Herausdrehung aus ihm*]."[1] A twisting free from Platonism into—what? Into a space lacking all the bounds, limits, measure previously installed by two and a half millennia of Western thought and language; into a space—or, rather, an abyss—in which all bounds would be crossed, all limits crossed out, all measure exceeded. In telling the story, Nietzsche twists free into the exorbitant, the immeasurable, the boundless—in a word: *das Masslose.*

Heidegger dates this event. He cites a letter written to Carl von

---

1. Martin Heidegger, *Nietzsche* (Pfullingen: Günther Neske, 1961), 1: 233.

Gersdorff just over a year before Nietzsche's final collapse on 3 January 1889. Near the beginning of the letter (dated 20 December 1887) Nietzsche writes: "In a significant sense my life stands right now at *high noon:* one door is closing, another opening." Nietzsche refers to his great task and passion and then adds, almost as if parenthetically: "In fact the desert surrounding me is monstrous." Heidegger concludes: "Here already are early signs of the last year of his thinking, the year in which everything about him radiates an excessive brilliance and in which therefore at the same time the boundless [*das Masslose*] advances out of the distance."[2] In his final creative year Nietzsche takes his final step, the reversal that twists free of Platonism; and *therefore at the same time,* says Heidegger, the boundless advances upon him. The excessive radiance of Nietzsche's last year, the brilliance with which he comes to see beyond Platonism, does not stop the advance of the boundless; rather, it is precisely then that, in the language of Nietzsche's letter, the desert surrounding him becomes ever more monstrous. Heidegger writes: "During the time when the overturning of Platonism became for Nietzsche a twisting free of it, madness befell him."[3] It is at this point, then, that Heidegger proceeds to retell the story of "How the 'True World' Finally Became a Fable," marking in the final episode that moment when Nietzsche no longer merely overturns Platonism but also twists free of it.

Well in advance of this renarration in which Heidegger's text "The Will to Power as Art" reaches its climax, Heidegger cites a remark from Nietzsche's early sketches for *The Birth of Tragedy:* "My philosophy an *inverted Platonism:* the further removed from true being, the purer, the more beautiful, the better it is. Living in *Schein* as goal." Heidegger notes: "This is an astonishing preview in the thinker of his entire later philosophical position, for during the last years of his creative life he labors at nothing else than this overturning of Platonism." And yet, Heidegger finds in the writings of the young Nietzsche *only* a preview, which he insists on rigorously distinguishing from the overturning that was to be attained in Nietzsche's final year: "Of course, we may not overlook the fact that the 'inverted Platonism' of his early period is enormously dif-

2. Ibid., 23. For the passage cited from Nietzsche's letter, see BKG III 5: 214.
3. Heidegger, *Nietzsche,* 1: 233.

ferent from the position finally attained in *Twilight of the Idols.*"[4] It is almost as if one could leap over those early texts on the way to the texts of the late 1880s.

Yet, suppose one were to resist that leap, at least deferring it long enough to formulate some preliminary questions. Then one would want to ask, first of all: What is the difference between the inversion of Platonism broached—in more ways than one—in *The Birth of Tragedy* and that which Nietzsche attains in his last year? Is it that the early texts only invert Platonism without twisting free of it? Is it simply a matter of their stopping short of that final move by which the hold of the fundamental Platonic distinction would be broken, of their continuing, despite the inversion, to circulate within the compass of that distinction? Do the early texts only venture in part what the final texts carry through completely?

What if, instead, it should turn out that from the beginning Nietzsche's thought is engaged in twisting free of Platonism, not only in *The Birth of Tragedy* but even in such earlier sketches as those from which Heidegger cites? What if these earlier texts not only were exposed to the advance of the boundless but also undertook *to think the boundless?* What if all that is gathered in *The Birth of Tragedy* should prove to have been written in a desert inhabited by monsters?

What if undertaking to think the boundless should prove inseparable from an engagement with Socrates? In that case, Nietzsche would prove to have twisted free of Platonism only in turning toward and engaging the principal figure inscribed, perhaps inextricably, in the Platonic texts, even if the reinscription in which that engagement would issue should prove to be one at which the Platonic texts only hint in the image of Socrates writing music.

In a reading addressed to these suppositions, one that would reopen Nietzsche's early texts in this direction, it is not to be presumed that the leap across to the final texts will simply have been avoided, even though those texts do not at all enter into the reading. For the very questions that orient such a reading are inseparable from the strategy by which Heidegger exposed Nietzsche's advance to the limit, the engagement of his thought at the limit of metaphysics. For a reading thus submitted, a double movement is

4. Ibid., 180. For the passage cited from Nietzsche, see III 3: 207.

required: returning to *The Birth of Tragedy* along the axis of the Heideggerian questions but also reading it at cross-purposes, slowly, carefully detaching it from that axis, reinscribing it elsewhere.

A double reading that would also be a double crossing.

The beginnings of such a reading, some preliminary indications, can also be assembled around the figure of crossing.

For *The Birth of Tragedy* not only marks various crossings but also—even if almost in silence, even if with a certain delay—enacts them.

Both the Apollinian and the Dionysian are marked as crossings that move beyond the everyday: to the world of beautiful images over which Apollo presides; or to the self-oblivion of the ecstatic state, as in the descent to Hades, as in crossing, in that direction, the river of Lethe.

The Apollinian and the Dionysian come to be crossed in a union as abysmal as that of the two sexes. They come to be crossed almost as animals or plants of different varieties, different species, can be crossed, either in reality or in imagination. Thus, it is a question of the birth of tragedy. Much of the text thus entitled is devoted to exposing and outlining the space of this birth, the space unfolded through it. Literally the space bounded by the orchestra and the proscenium, the chorus and the stage, the space of tragedy is a space in which a certain manifestation comes to pass, a space of disclosure. It is a space that is also linked to time, to history, in a relation of which *The Birth of Tragedy* attempts to take the measure, charting the birth, death, and rebirth of tragedy. And yet, if among the Greeks it was tragedy that was born from the crossing of Apollinian and Dionysian, this birth testifies not only to the depths of their needs but also to their fortune. For in crossing variant species there is always the risk of producing monsters; and indeed in *The Birth of Tragedy* there are more monsters than one would ever have thought.

One of them is named Socrates. He crosses tragedy, not by pairing it with still another, but by thwarting it, contravening it, opposing it to the very point of death. Socrates reduces that space of disclosure that is the space of tragedy, and through this reduction he crosses out tragedy, in advance, from the history of metaphysics, from what Nietzsche at first calls simply Socratism and, later, Platonism.

Thus, tragedy is also set aside from Christianity, that "Platonism for 'the people' " (VI 2: 4). Thus is prepared the opposition between Dionysus and the Crucified.

Also there is prepared—in the very unfolding of the Socratic reduction—a rebirth of tragedy. The question is inevitable: Does the rebirth of tragedy only reverse again the opposition? Or does it broach a new crossing of tragedy with its opposite? What of the music-practicing Socrates promised in Nietzsche's text?

The promise is not made without a certain slippage, and the figure is haunted by a certain undecidability. Emblems of the heterogeneity of Nietzsche's text, of its boundlessness.

It is because of the peculiar heterogeneity of *The Birth of Tragedy* that reference to other, related texts is imperative. First of all, there are the various preliminary drafts that were revised and put together to form most of the text of *The Birth of Tragedy*.[5] The first of these are the two public lectures that Nietzsche presented at Basel early in 1870: "The Greek Music Drama" and "Socrates and Tragedy";[6] the latter would eventually form most of sections 11–14 of the published work. If one is to believe what Nietzsche wrote just afterwards to Erwin Rohde, the reception of this lecture was portentous of the furor that would erupt after the publication of *The Birth of Tragedy* itself: "I have given a lecture here on 'Socrates and Tragedy,' which excited terror and incomprehension." Yet Nietzsche himself was only spurred on with his monstrous project; the letter continues: "Knowledge, art, and philosophy are now growing together so much in me that I shall in any case give birth to a centaur one day" (BKG II 1: 95).[7] Second among the preliminary drafts is the text of a lecture course on *Oedipus Tyrannos* that Nietzsche gave during the summer semester of 1870;[8] this is the

5. The relation between the various drafts and their relation to the published text is discussed in detail by M. S. Silk and J. P. Stern, *Nietzsche on Tragedy* (Cambridge: Cambridge University Press, 1981), 31–61.

6. "Das griechische Musikdrama" and "Socrates und die Tragoedie" (III 2: 3–22, 23–41). Nietzsche had a reworked version of the latter privately printed in 1871 (III 2: 93–132). Cf. Nietzsche's letter of 7 June 1871 to Rohde (BKG II 1: 197).

7. About the same time he wrote to Paul Deussen that "Socrates and Tragedy" has been understood here as a chain of paradoxes and has aroused hatred and anger in some" (BKG II 1: 98).

8. "Einleitung zu den Vorlesungen über Sophocles Oedipus rex" (W 17: 291–325).

text that marks the first public reference to the duality of Apollinian and Dionysian. The third of the drafts, "The Dionysian
Worldview,"[9] was written in the summer of 1870 and was to provide the basis for much of what is found in the first ten sections of
The Birth of Tragedy. In addition to these drafts, there are several
other manuscripts that, though in a sense more marginal to The
Birth of Tragedy, nonetheless have an important bearing upon it;
among these are the well-known texts "Philosophy in the Tragic
Age of the Greeks" and "On Truth and Lies in a Nonmoral Sense"
(II 2: 293–366, 367–84), as well as a little-noticed early fragment
on Schopenhauer;[10] and the lecture courses on Preplatonic philosophy, on Plato, and on Greek literature that Nietzsche gave in Basel
in the early 1870s.[11] There is, in addition, the mass of notebook
entries from this period, now collected in volume III 3 of the Colli-
Montinari edition. To say nothing of the very remarkable retrospective texts of the 1880s, such as the "Attempt at a Self-
Critique" prepared for the new edition of The Birth of Tragedy (III 1:
5–16) and the relevant section of Ecce Homo (VI 3: 307–13).

Reading The Birth of Tragedy requires crossing it with these
other texts, which serve sometimes to fill its gaps, sometimes to
stabilize its vacillations and resolve its undecidables, sometimes to
displace and reopen questions about what seems secure in the text
published in 1872.

Reading this text also requires crossing it with something else,
submitting both what is said and its saying to exigencies that can
have arisen only in the aftermath of Nietzsche's work, through the
Heideggerian reading and all that it has opened up. Double crossing Nietzsche's text, then, with a kind of posthumous double.

9. "Die dionysische Weltanschauung" (III 2: 43–69). In November 1870
Nietzsche wrote to Erwin Rohde: "In the summer I wrote, for my own benefit, a
long essay, 'On the Dionysian Worldview,' so as to keep myself calm as the storm
brewed" (BKG II 1: 159–60). A slightly altered version of this essay, under the
title "Die Geburt des tragischen Gedankens" (III 2: 71–91), was given to Cosima
Wagner for Christmas 1870.
10. "Fragment einer Kritik der Schopenhauerischen Philosophie" (M 1: 392–
401).
11. "Die Vorplatonischen Philosophen" (Summer 1872, 1873, 1876) (W 19);
"Einleitung in das Studium der platonischen Dialoge" (Winter 1871–72, Winter
1873–74, Summer 1876) (W 19); "Geschichte der griechischen Litteratur"
(Winter 1874–75, Summer 1875) (W 18).

But then writing across it still another text, reinscribing it but also crossing it out, erasing it, adding to its saying the unsaying that what is said requires. Producing, then, a text that is something of a double of *The Birth of Tragedy,* a phantom, a spirit, that has already begun to haunt it.

1 | A P O L L O —

Shining Phantasy

a

Later his writing will turn on itself, again and again reflecting, dividing, displacing itself. The spacing will be most direct in the various discourses on reading and writing. Thus the discourse "Why I Write Such Good Books" (*Ecce Homo*) turns upon those books, supplementing them in such a way as to inscribe a certain distance between reading and writing, between those books and their "modern" readers:

> That today one does not hear me, that today one does not know to take ·
> from me, is not only comprehensible, it even seems right to me. . . .
> With this feeling of distance, how could I wish to be read by those "moderns" whom I know! (VI 3: 296–97)

Thus, Nietzsche withdraws from modernity what he has written, reserving his books for their posthumous birth.

Such a discourse is also found in *Thus Spoke Zarathustra*, identified as such by the title of the section "On Reading and Writing." Again it is a matter of withdrawal from the reader, at least from those idle readers who do not know how hard it is to understand something that one has written with one's blood:

> Of all that is written I love only what a man writes with his blood. Write with blood: and you will experience that blood is spirit. It is not easily possible to understand the blood of another [*fremdes Blut*]: I hate the reading idlers. Whoever knows the reader will henceforth do nothing for the reader. Another century of readers—and the spirit itself will stink. (VI 1: 44)

Here the inscription is neither external (another book, as in the case of *Ecce Homo*) nor subsequent (as in the case of a belated preface) but occurs within the book itself, as a certain turning of the book on itself. Yet, it goes almost without saying that this book for all and none is anything but a *book itself*, that it is, rather, a writing divided from itself, manifoldly self-displacing—first of all, simply by being a book of *speeches*.

The belated preface that Nietzsche wrote in 1886 for *The Dawn* is different. Neither simply part of the book itself nor part of another book, it hovers at the threshold. Neither does it fail to offer the book to certain readers, though not without warnings and demands. This preface exposes the author of the book, declaring him a subterranean tunneler, a mole, one who has since returned almost as if from the dead, one who now betrays that he has also remained—who is still, fourteen years after *The Birth of Tragedy*—a philologist, that is to say "a teacher of slow reading." He is declared to be also one who writes slowly, one with the taste "no longer to write anything that does not bring to despair every sort of man who is 'in a hurry.'" The reader too must keep his distance. He too must practice philology, that venerable art that "teaches to read *well*, that is, to read slowly, deeply, looking cautiously behind and ahead [*rück- und vorsichtig*], with reservations, with doors left open, with delicate eyes and fingers" (V 1: 3, 9). Thus turning on *The Dawn*, the Preface inscribes the space of its reading and writing.

The Birth of Tragedy too will receive a belated preface. Nietzsche will write it in the same year as the Preface to *The Dawn*. But though in the 1886 edition of *The Birth of Tragedy* it will be set in the place of a preface, preceding the book itself as well as the original title page, it will not be entitled *Vorrede*, nor *Vorwort*, but rather "Attempt at a Self-Critique" ("Versuch einer Selbstkritik"). The title expresses the distance separating this belated "preface" from the book that it will come to preface; this distance cannot but compound everything that is troublesome about prefacing, about a text that would be outside the text that it can properly precede only by having been written afterwards and by not being outside it. Indeed, this "preface" turns on the book from a distance that none of Nietzsche's other belated prefaces attempt, a distance found perhaps in only one other such text, namely, the section of "Why I Write Such Good Books" directed at *The Birth of Tragedy*. It goes without saying that today one cannot read *The Birth of Tragedy* without discussing these two supplemental texts. And yet, precisely because of their distance from the book itself, a certain distinction must be observed. Even if they cannot simply be bound at the end of the book, there will be certain advantages gained by deferring consideration of the way in which they inscribe, retro-spectively, the space of reading and writing *The Birth of Tragedy.*

For it is not as though they come to supply an inscription that was simply lacking in the book that Nietzsche published in 1872. On the contrary, the book in its initial form begins with a foreword (*Vorwort*); or, rather, it begins by deferring its beginning so as to make place for the prefatory text, which itself, on the other hand, openly betrays that—as so often with prefaces, even in a sense nec-essarily—it was written after the completion of the book itself. Its very title is such as to address it to a reader, to a single, privileged reader: "Foreword to Richard Wagner." It addresses that reader by anticipating his reception of the book: "I picture the moment when you, my highly respected friend, will receive this writing." It addresses him further by portraying what might occur to that reader at the moment when, opening the book, he is on the verge of beginning to read: "how, perhaps after an evening walk in the winter snow, you will behold Prometheus unbound on the title page, read my name, and be convinced at once that, whatever this writing may contain, the author has something serious and urgent to say" (III 1: 19). The voice addressing Wagner in the Foreword assumes finally the distance of the third person with respect to its addressee only in order to conclude by announcing in first person the dedication of this writing to him.

Nietzsche also sent the book to Wagner, even before it was bound, sent it as a slightly belated Christmas gift (*Weihnachtsgabe*). Accompanying this copy, which showed the unchained, unbound (*entfesselt*) Prometheus on the title page, there was a letter with the promise: "In a short time I shall send you and your wife bound copies [*gebundene Exemplare*]." The letter not only announces that the book is a gift to Wagner (who is addressed as *Verehrtester Meister*) but also outlines the circuit of giving, the exchange, in which it was inscribed: "On every page you will find that I am only trying to thank you for everything you have given me; only doubt seizes me as to whether I have always correctly received what you gave me" (BKG II 1: 272). Wagner is the privileged reader because the book is a gift to him, given as thanks to him, in exchange for what he had given Nietzsche, hence with a certain equivalence, even if Nietzsche was concerned that he might not have received correctly all that Wagner gave and that consequently he might not be able to repay Wagner with the full equivalent of what the latter had given him.[1] A draft of another letter to Wagner—or, perhaps, of the same one—written presumably on the same day defines the terms of the exchange even more rigorously, saying what it is said would not be said in Wagner's presence: "In your presence [*Vor Ihnen*], my esteemed friend and master, I will at least refrain from confessing that everything I have to say here about the birth of Greek tragedy has been said more beautifully, clearly, and convincingly by you" (BKG II 1: 270–71). It is a matter not just of equivalence but of virtual identity of content, of repeating what "has been said more beautifully, clearly, and convincingly" by the master. Wagner is the privileged reader because his reading alone—that reading whose threshold the Foreword anticipates—constitutes the reception of the gift as which the writing is offered. Even though when Wagner receives the book it is still unbound. Even if, sixteen years later, his copy could belatedly have been bound with those supplemental texts that, inscribing a different space for the book, would in a sense drive Wagner from that space:

To be fair to *The Birth of Tragedy* (1872), one must forget a few things. Its effect and its fascination were due to what was wrong with it—its practical application to Wagnerism. . . . A psychologist might still add that what I heard as a young man listening to Wagnerian music had nothing at all to do with Wagner. (VI 3: 307, 311)

And yet, the "Foreword to Richard Wagner" does not entirely forego addressing other readers and inscribing, even if in the broadest strokes, the space of their reading of *The Birth of Tragedy*.[2] But it addresses them only indirectly, only by referring to them

1. There is a draft of another forward that Nietzsche wrote in Lugano in February 1871. It too is entitled "Vorwort an Richard Wagner." In this draft Nietzsche begins by expressing the solidarity between his view and Wagner's regarding "Greek cheerfulness," their agreement that a distinction must be drawn between "a true and a false concept of 'Greek cheerfulness'" and that by means of the latter concept one could never attain "insight into the essence of tragedy." Having thus expressed the solidarity, Nietzsche then assigns *The Birth of Tragedy* to Wagner: "Therefore, the following discussion of the origin and goal of the tragic work of art is due [belongs—*gebührt*] to you" (III 3: 367).

2. In a letter written in mid-February 1872, just after the publication of *The Birth of Tragedy*, Nietzsche tells Rohde that he and Jacob Burckhardt are ideal readers for the book: "You and he—you two together—really supply the ideal of the correct reader" (BKG II 2: 294).

in the course of addressing Wagner, putting at a distance the "scruples, excitements, and misunderstandings" that *The Birth of Tragedy* will occasion in these others, putting them at a distance by imagining the scene of Wagner's reception of the book. These others, Nietzsche says, would be mistaken if their reading were to be oriented to the contrast between patriotic excitement (provoked by the Franco-Prussian War) and aesthetic enthusiasm; but "with a real reading of this writing [*bei einem wirklichen Lesen dieser Schrift*]," they would discover to their astonishment what a seriously German problem is treated here. But—Nietzsche addresses them again, still indirectly, still addressing Wagner, though beginning to drift toward the third-person announcement of the dedication—for these other readers "it will perhaps be scandalous for an aesthetic problem to be taken so seriously." These others, for whom art may be no more than an inconsequential tinkling of bells, must still learn something if they are to be readers at all, something that Nietzsche now declares in a single, almost deafening stroke: they must learn—as Nietzsche has learned from his sublime predecessor on this path—"that art is the highest task and the genuinely metaphysical activity of this life." This stroke will resound throughout *The Birth of Tragedy*, resound as the opposition that will both structure the book and perpetually threaten it from within by putting into question the very space of its writing.

The "Foreword to Richard Wagner" not only binds that writing to Wagner's presence (the author "could write down only something corresponding to this presence [*nur etwas dieser Gegenwart Entsprechendes*]") but also describes it as a writing infused with contemplative delight (*beschauliche Wonne*), even though done "amid the terrors and sublimities [*in den Schrecken und Erhabenheiten*] of the war that had just broken out." One can hardly not call up another image that will soon be drawn from Schopenhauer in order to suggest what is granted by the Apollinian world of images, the contemplative delight that it offers in the midst of the storm: "Just as on a stormy sea that, unbounded in all directions, raises and drops mountainous waves, howling, a sailor sits in a boat and trusts in his frail bark . . ." (III 1: 24).

Later Nietzsche recognizes that the frail bark cannot but have capsized, casting the Apollinian sailor into the abysmal sea, exposing him to its roaring terror. By virtue of what will have been written, the contemplative delight with which it was to have been written cannot but have been interrupted, double crossed by that very writing. As, among the Greeks, Dionysus had once—indeed more than once and finally once and for all—interrupted the reign of Apollo.

b

Not only gods but also monsters and giants haunt the opening pages of *The Birth of Tragedy*. From the very beginning everything is oriented to the duality of Apollinian and Dionysian, or, rather, to the monstrous opposition (*ungeheurer Gegensatz*) between these two forces that will be shown to have empowered the entire history of Greek art. The Apollinian dream world is portrayed as offering delight in images, in the magnificent figures of the gods, which, according to Lucretius, first appeared to men in dreams. For a time one is like the Greek sculptor who beholds the enchanting frames of superhuman beings (*übermenschlicher Wesen*) and has only, like the poet described by Hans Sachs, to interpret, in and through the artwork that he fashions, what has appeared in his dream. Even in such excess, even in the superhuman, one takes delight as long as another sort of excess does not intervene, that of the frenzy (*Rausch*) that oversteps all limits; or, rather, as long as that monstrous excess does not *return,* for Apollinian culture will always have had first to overthrow an empire of Titans and to slay monsters (*Ungethüme*) (III 1: 33). When it intervenes, when it returns, man is seized by a monstrous terror (*das ungeheure Grausen*)—and yet, also by a joyful enchantment (*die wonnevolle Verzückung*) in which something supernatural (*etwas Uebernatürliches*) sounds forth from him, as, feeling himself now a god, he walks about no less enchanted than those gods he saw in his dreams.

Yet, it is not only with contemplative delight in these marvelous figures that Nietzsche's book begins. Even if, as he tells Wagner, there are on every page signs of such delight, there is also a certain discursiveness, a dimension of theoretical discourse that is not simply assimilable to Apollinian contemplation. For it is a matter, not of art, but of aesthetic science. The time has come to read the opening sentence of the book:

We shall have gained much for aesthetic science [*die aesthetische Wissenschaft*], once we grasp not merely by logical insight but with the immediate certainty of intuition [*Anschauung*] that the continuous development of art is bound up with the duality of *Apollinian* and *Dionysian;* in a way similar to that in which procreation depends on the twofoldedness of the sexes [*Zweiheit der Geschlechter*], involving perpetual strife with only periodically intervening reconciliations. (III 1: 21)

Even if art has been declared the genuinely metaphysical—here already the pronouncement of this identity resounds, is set resonating by the tone sounded, as it will be again and again—this opening is such as to set Nietzsche's book at a certain distance from that point of identity, decentering it, driving it into a space that will never cease reopening within it. It is a matter of aesthetics, of contributing to the science of aesthetics. Directed toward a theoretical presentation of art, such science broaches an opposition that the entirety of *The Birth of Tragedy*—even beyond what is outlined in the opening passage—will be devoted to establishing, an opposition that itself is obliquely opposed to the resounding identity: the opposition is that between theory and art, between what will be determined as the Socratic project and, in the highest instance, Greek tragedy. Although, well beyond the opening, much about Nietzsche's text will have the effect of binding it to the side of theory, the operation of this opposition back upon the text—to say nothing of the resounding pronouncement of identity—will inevitably have the effect of dividing Nietzsche's text from itself; such is no doubt one of the reasons that by 1886 *The Birth of Tragedy* seemed to Nietzsche quite "an impossible book" (III 1: 7). In this connection one could compare its character to that which Nietzsche attributed to philology in his inaugural lecture "Homer and Classical Philology" (1869): a manifold character, lacking an abstract unity, an aggregate bound together only by the name (II 1: 249). From the beginning *The Birth of Tragedy* is even more heterogeneous, more lacking in stability, more prone to dislocation by the operation of its own dynamics.

Even in its opening, Nietzsche's text is released somewhat from the side of theory, beginning to slide across the space of the opposition, even if—perhaps for a long time—somewhat aimlessly. Since it is directed toward a theoretical presentation *of art,* it must arrive, not merely at logical insight, but at immediate certainty of intuition. The presentation cannot be such as merely to transcribe logical insight, expressing thus a conceptual grasp of the development of art, but must also be informed by an immediate, intuitive grasp. This imperative will be continually confirmed by what *The Birth of Tragedy* will bring to light, confirmed as corresponding to a certain irreducibility of art, to the impossibility of reinscribing it within the order of concepts without thereby reenacting that destruction of art that was first enacted in the origination of theoretical, i.e., Socratic, philosophy. In Nietzsche's text it will be primarily a question neither of concepts nor of intuitions but rather of figures. There is a gesture toward Apollo even before he is named in the text.

Nietzsche appeals to the Greeks, to their intuition of art (*Kunstanschauung*). The appeal to intuition addresses, in effect, the question of situating the Greek insight into art with respect to the opposition between theory and art. There are other texts roughly contemporaneous with *The Birth of Tragedy* that indicate quite explicitly that the Greek insight into art is itself somehow to be situated on the side of art, not of theory; or, rather, that such insight precedes the very separation of theory over against art. For example, a fragment from 1869 refers to the "wonderful time when the arts still developed without the artist's inventing finished theories of art [*fertige Kunsttheorien*]" (III 3: 22).[3] *The Birth of Tragedy* decides the question almost as directly by indicating how these "highest of all teachers," as the Greeks will later be called (III 1: 125), make their intuition of art perceptible (*vernehmbar machen*): "not, to be sure, in concepts, but in the penetratingly clear figures of their gods [*Gestalten ihrer Götterwelt*]" (III 1: 21). In these figures they make again perceptible what they once intuited and somehow expressed in these figures, make it perceptible to those today capable of insight (*dem Einsichtigen*). It will be a matter, then, of attending to these figures, recoverable largely from Greek texts, indeed mostly from texts of Greek art, in order to reawaken through these figures such insight into art as the Greeks once achieved. The complexity of such recovery is thus already broached: to mention only one aspect, it is a matter of recovering the Greek experience of art by a way that begins with the experi-

---

3. Another fragment from the same year situates the separation in a way that concurs with the analyses later in *The Birth of Tragedy:* "Euripides is the first dramatist who follows a consciously entertained aesthetics [*der einer bewussten Aesthetik folgt*]" (III 3: 37).

ence of Greek art, with figures whose presentation is bound to Greek art and, hence, subject to all the difficulties that beset the attempt at originary access to Greek art.[4] *The Birth of Tragedy* is to transcribe a certain attunement to these figures, a certain movement both from them and through them, an enactment of a certain figural disclosure.

Only two gods, Apollo and Dionysus, figure primarily in the disclosure; whatever disclosive significance might accrue to other gods will prove to depend on their relation to Apollo or Dionysus, on their capacity to represent (in a sense that will have to be determined) Apollo or Dionysus. What is, then, to be disclosed through the figures of these two gods? At the outset Nietzsche names what is to be disclosed or, rather, merely transfers to that duality the names of the two gods through which the disclosure is to be effected: the duality is that of Apollinian and Dionysian. Thus are named the driving forces, the impulses, to which the development of art is bound (*Kunsttriebe*), the basic artistic energies (*künstlerische Mächte*) (cf. III 1: 26). Nietzsche stresses that the opposition is a *monstrous* opposition (*ein ungeheurer Gegensatz*), that is, at once natural and unnatural, a certain divergence from nature within nature. This opposition is, in turn, reflected by the opposition that was decisive in the history of Greek art:

Through Apollo and Dionysus, the two art deities of the Greeks, we come to recognize that in the Greek world there existed a monstrous opposition, in origin and aims, between the art of sculpture [*Kunst des Bildners*], the Apollinian, and the nonimagistic art of music [*unbildliche Kunst der Musik*], as that of Dionysus. (III 1: 21)

The opposition is thus determined primarily by the productive relation to images. Yet, it is not a simple opposition but already in the very opening of Nietzsche's text is marked as operative at three somewhat different levels: as an opposition (1) that was operative in the history of Greek art; as an opposition (2) in origin and aims between the form of art that produces images and the form that is

4. Nietzsche does not underestimate the problem of access to Greek art, for example, the problem involved in the fact that access to Greek drama is primarily through texts. In the lecture of 1870 entitled "The Greek Music Drama" he says: "In particular, I maintain that the Aeschylus and Sophocles known to us are known to us only as textbook poets, as librettists, that is, that they are quite unknown to us" (III 2: 7).

nonimagistic; and as an opposition (3) between the two impulses, the two artistic energies, that underlie these two forms of art both in general and in their particular occurrences in the history of Greek art.

Nietzsche stresses the force of this opposition between forces, stresses that it is monstrous. In the history of Greek art the two impulses were, for the most part, in open conflict, dissension (*Zwiespalt*), and yet precisely in their dissension they continually incited one another to new and more powerful births. Perpetuated through the incitement, theirs is a dissension "which the common word 'art' only seemingly bridges [*nur scheinbar überbrückt*]" (III 1: 21). The opposition is not one between species to be united under a generic term but rather is such as to threaten the very unity of the word *art,* leaving its operation in suspense in such a way as to jeopardize the very coherence of the identification of Apollinian and Dionysian as art impulses. The dissension generated is not, then, one to be readily mastered by logic and a language governed simply thereby. To tame such a monster, more is required than simply reenclosing it within those logical, allegedly natural circles that it will already have violated at birth.

And yet, the unity that is threatened, the coherence of *art,* does not simply precede the threat; that is, it is not as though there is first somehow unity, which then comes to be threatened. For while Nietzsche insists that the two impulses run parallel to one another (*gehen neben einander*) in such dissension as to threaten the unity of the word *art,* there are also indications, on the other hand, that that unity itself is in a sense constituted by the very parallelism that threatens to disrupt it. Thus the following note from 1870–71: "The parallelism [*Nebeneinander*] of Apollo and Dionysus, only a short time—is the time of the artwork" (III 3: 162).

Nietzsche draws explicitly the analogy between this opposition and that of the two sexes: perpetual strife with only periodically intervening reconciliations. The difference between Apollinian and Dionysian is no less dissentient—nor less complex—than sexual difference.

The complexity of the analogy itself is in play from the outset. Not only are the two sexes represented, on the side of art, by two male figures, but also there is told, to say the least, a curious history of the affair between these figures. They incite—or charm, entice (*reizen*)—each other to give birth, though by the series of births the strife between Apollo and Dionysus is only perpetuated. They remain—but for the moment of incitement—separated, remain in discord (*Zwiespalt*), producing only bastard offspring. Until, finally, "a metaphysical miracle" supervenes to join them in what would have seemed an impossible bond. The issue of this bond is legitimate; it is equally Dionysian and Apollinian. What is the character of this bond produced by metaphysical miracle and productive of Attic tragedy? One of the texts preparatory for *The Birth of Tragedy* characterizes it as a fusion: when these opposites come finally to generate tragedy, they "appear fused [*verschmolzen erscheinen*]" (III 2: 45). Certain notes from 1870–71 describe the bond as a union.[5] *The Birth of Tragedy* itself, in its opening, characterizes the bond in a way more consonant with the sexual analogy: they appear coupled (*gepaart*) with one another and in this coupling (*Paarung*) generate Attic tragedy. Later, in one of the texts that closes the era of *The Birth of Tragedy* by glancing back along its trajectory, Nietzsche will characterize the bond also—even if at a certain distance—as a crossing (*Kreuzung*).[6]

5. One such note, quite contemporaneous with the composition of *The Birth of Tragedy,* parallels closely the initial statement of that work: "Two basic impulses of Hellenic art are recognizable, the Apollinian and the Dionysian. They unite [*vereinigen sich*] in order to produce a new form of art, that of tragic conception [*des tragischen Gedankens*]" (III 3: 214). Another note from the same period (1871) opposes the view that would correlate the difference between the Greek world and the modern world with that between the plastic arts (Apollinian) and music (Dionysian): "It is quite erroneous to suppose that the Greek world is characterized by the plastic arts and the modern by music. The Greek world had, rather, the full union [*die volle Vereinigung*] of Dionysian and Apollinian" (III 3: 330).

6. The text is *Richard Wagner in Bayreuth* (1876), the fourth of the *Untimely Meditations*. Though Nietzsche does not mention Apollinian and Dionysian and though clearly in this text it is not simply a matter of repetition, the affinity to that duality is unmistakably marked. Referring to Wagner's expression of the experience of taking art so seriously that one is tempted to take life too easily, to find the dream almost more true than waking actuality, Nietzsche writes of the dithyrambic dramatist, who, amidst the everyday, must feel like one awake in a world of sleepwalkers: "But this sensation is characteristically crossed when to the brightness of this exuberance there is joined a quite different impulse, the longing to descend from the heights into the depths, the living desire for the earth, for the joy of communication. . . . The crossing assumed here is the actual miracle in the soul of the dithyrambic dramatist; and if his nature can be conceptually grasped anywhere, it must be here. For the creative moments in his art are produced by the tension occasioned by this crossing of sensations, when the uncanny and exuberant sensation of surprise and amazement at the world is coupled with the ardent

If the opposition between Apollinian and Dionysian is monstrous, then the birth of tragedy from the crossing of those opposites is for Nietzsche something abysmal, as little accessible to reason as is the attachment of generation to the duality of the sexes. Let me cite a note from 1870–71:

> That nature attached the origination of tragedy to those two basic impulses, the Apollinian and the Dionysian, we should consider just as much an abyss of reason [*ein Abgrund der Vernunft*] as the arrangement by which nature attaches propagation to the duality of the sexes, something that always seemed astonishing to the great Kant. The common mystery is, in particular, how from two principles alien to one another [*zwei einander feindlichen Principien*] something new can arise in which those conflicting impulses appear as unity. (III 3: 187)

The question—to formulate it provisionally, that is, all too quickly, without the precautions that it will eventually require—will be: how to think this abysmal unity without reducing either the monstrosity of the opposition or the abysmal crossing in which and as which tragedy arises.

And yet, does the space of tragedy not involve another dimension, one of depth, of separation between art and nature, the spread of mimesis? If it is a matter of recovering the Greek insight into art, must Nietzsche not at least move through that global determination of art as mimesis that emerged with the separation between theory and art, the determination that was established by Plato and Aristotle precisely in the aftermath of Greek tragedy and that henceforth governed virtually all theory of art, all "aesthetic science"? Must the way to the Greek intuition of art not pass through the concept of art as imitation of nature, even if only to produce eventually a dislocation of that concept? Is this not why, as a contemporaneous note says, "aesthetics makes sense only as natural science" (III 3: 421)?

It might appear that Nietzsche has already broken with the mimetic concept of art in the very opening of *The Birth of Tragedy,*

---

longing to approach this same world as a lover. . . . What has hitherto been invisible and inward escapes into the sphere of the visible and becomes appearance; what was hitherto only visible flees into the dark sea of sound: *thus by seeking to hide itself, nature reveals the essence of its opposites*. . . . A dream appearance . . . expands as the expression of a wholly heroic exuberant will, of a rapturous going-under and cessation of will: —thus arises tragedy" (IV 1: 42–44).

in posing Dionysian art as nonimagistic. And yet, it is in this very context that Nietzsche reaffirms—even if with a certain caution—the mimetic conception of art: "Over against these immediate art-states [*Kunstzustände*] of nature, every artist is an 'imitator' ['*Nachahmer*'] . . ." (III 1: 26). Apollinian and Dionysian are, then, first of all "artistic energies that burst forth from nature itself *without the mediation of the human artist*" (III 1: 26). They are states of nature by which nature will in a sense always have anticipated art, states of nature in which there is already, in the direction of art, a certain monstrous break with nature, complicating the classical opposition between nature and art even before the advent of the human artist. The artist—every artist—produces an imitation of one or the other of these impulses, these art-states of nature. Even the Dionysian artist, though his art is nonimagistic, produces nonetheless an imitation of nature, or more precisely, of a state that bursts forth from nature. Indeed, the problem of Dionysian art lies precisely in the difference thus posited between imitation and image. This difference will prove to generate the coordinates of the space of tragedy.

C

The Apollinian is, then, first of all, an artistic energy that bursts forth from nature prior to the advent of the artist. It is a natural state presupposed by Apollinian art, that is, by all imagistic art (*bildende Kunst*) and an important part of poetry; such art would arise precisely through and as an imitation of this prior state. In the most telling phrase, the Apollinian is, first of all, an art-impulse of nature (*Kunsttrieb der Natur*). It is as though nature itself already contained the transition from nature to art, even if holding it in a certain reserve; or, rather, it is as though nature and art crossed in a region that would be neither simply nature nor yet art, a kind of natural proto-art or proto-artistic nature. Nietzsche identifies this proto-artistic Apollinian with the creative impulse operative and manifest in dreams, identifies them at least to the extent of proposing to *think* the Apollinian *as* the dream world. More precisely, he refers to it both as impulse, energy, power (*Trieb, Macht*) and as state or condition (*Zustand*). The distinction reflects a certain complexity that Nietzsche never quite makes explicit: the Apollinian is not simply detached production, indifferent to what is produced, unattracted to those images. Rather, as the impulse that produces the dream world, the Apollinian is also a state of absorption in that world, in its play of images, even though it will prove essential to the Apollinian that such absorption always observes a certain limit. What one might call, then, the double orientation toward the image—producing it and being absorbed in it—makes all the more appropriate Nietzsche's approach to the Apollinian by way of a characterization of the dream-image.[7]

And yet, it is not simply a matter of dream analysis either in general or in reference to the Greeks ("we can speak of their *dreams* only conjecturally"—III 1: 27). What is to be recovered is a certain Greek insight into art, an insight that for the Greeks was bound up with certain of the arts, with a certain direction of artistic development that mirrored itself in Apollo. The god, produced by Apollinian art, was, in turn, an image of the very impulse underlying all such art. For Nietzsche it is, then, a matter of attending to the figure of the god as handed down in Greek art and of bringing into play the capacity of this figure to mirror both the proto-artistic Apollinian impulse and Apollinian art.

If Nietzsche had included in *The Birth of Tragedy* a more philologically oriented discussion of Homer,[8] then he would presumably have elaborated through a more direct interpretation of Greek epic poetry those particular features of the god that mirror the proto-artistic impulse and its artistic sequel. Lacking such a discussion, I shall resort to the expedient of gathering up a few things said of Apollo in *The Iliad* and in the *Homeric Hymn to Apollo,* linking an episode of the great epic with various attributions and epithets. Such a way of underwriting Nietzsche's text would have to be considered somewhat retrospective and partial, were not the very order of vision so utterly in question here, to say nothing of completeness.[9]

---

7. A note written between 1870 and 1872 reads: "Purely Apollinian: effect [*Wirkung*] as image" (III 3: 232).

8. It seems that he considered such an addition, since one of the notebook entries from the time of the composition of *The Birth of Tragedy* reads: "I want also to add something philologically to the writing [*Schrift*], e.g., a section on metrics, on Homer" (III 3: 217).

9. Ever since Ulrich von Wilamowitz-Möllendorff's vitriolic review "Philology of the Future!" (1872) ("Zukunftphilologie!"—reprinted in *Der Streit um Nietzsches "Geburt der Tragödie,"* ed. K. Grunder [Hildesheim: Georg Olms,

So, a few names and deeds of Apollo, drawn from Apollinian art, grouped around three foci. First of all, the epithet that became virtually part of his proper name: φοῖβος 'Απόλλων bespeaks brightness, radiance, shining. Nietzsche calls Apollo the "shining one" (der "Scheinende"). Next, from The Iliad the story of Apollo's

---

1969], 27–55), Nietzsche has been attacked for his lack of philological rigor in elaborating the characters of Apollo and Dionysus, for skewing the portraits of the gods in certain directions supportive of his own "views." The same charges, though not quite the same tone, are brought forth again in the recent study by Silk and Stern, Nietzsche on Tragedy. These authors note, for example, that "the god's [Apollo's] traditional association with music is not something that he is eager to emphasize," and that the healing and the self-restraint associated with Apollo are given "a metaphysical meaning" (170). They conclude their inventory thus: "Finally, three new aspects are added. Nietzsche's Apollo is a god of dreams, god of appearance and 'illusion,' god of visual art, and these three related functions are subsequently combined in terms of an Apolline 'world of visual imagery' (Bilderwelt). The three functions represent Nietzsche's extension in its most extreme form. There is no ancient authority for them, in any ordinary sense of the word: he has invented them. They have, however, one feature in common with his more moderate innovations: they sharpen the antithesis with Dionysus" (170–71). It is hardly necessary to observe that these charges are quite imprecise in reference to the developments in Nietzsche's text: Nietzsche does not propose that Apollo is the god of dreams in the sense that, for example, Ares can be called the god of war; the sense in which Apollo is portrayed as the god of the visual arts is hardly self-evident and, in any case, quite complex; and the engagement of the semantics of Schein in Nietzsche's discourse is, Wilamowitz notwithstanding, anything but a simple pun (cf. "Zukunftphilologie," 34; also Silk and Stern, 406). What is more objectionable is the way in which such charges tacitly involve a reduction of the structure of Nietzsche's discourse, as though it were simply a matter of establishing a philologically complete inventory of the god's features and then determining the Apollinian on the basis of such an inventory; as though it were not a matter of recovering through the figure of the god a certain understanding of art that is made perceptible in that figure; as though it were not a matter of movement—itself peculiarly Apollinian, even if problematically—through the image of the god to an impulse that it mirrors. Once the problematic is formulated even in these terms, which remain preliminary, questions of completeness, of skewing, etc., must be posed at a level much more complex than that at which such discussions have usually moved.

It should be noted that, despite their charges, Silk and Stern in the end grant a certain "general validity" to the Apollinian/Dionysian opposition: "Nevertheless, in spite of all these objections, the antithesis can still stand: it has a general validity and (in Nietzsche's favor) a greater validity for the archaic period, when tragedy was born, than for the fifth century, when the two deities and their attributes seem to have been subject to a certain convergence." Silk and Stern add a citation from Plutarch "which looks . . . forward to Nietzsche's own version of the antithesis" (184).

deeds in coming to the aid of Aeneas.[10] Homer tells how Diomedes, lord of the war cry, attacks Aeneas, intending to kill him and take his armor, even though Diomedes knows full well that Aeneas is under the protection of Apollo. Fearing not even the god, Diomedes charges at Aeneas three times, but each time Apollo intervenes and beats back Diomedes' shield. When on his fourth try Diomedes charges upon Aeneas like a god (δαίμονι ἶσος), Apollo raises a bloodcurdling cry:

> "Look out! Give way!
> Enough of this, this craze to vie with god!
> Our kind, immortals of the open sky,
> will never be like yours, earth-faring men."[11]

Diomedes backs away slightly to avoid the wrath of far-shooting (ἑκατηβόλος) Apollo. Seizing the opportunity, Apollo snatches up Aeneas and speeds him off to sacred Pergamos, where he is then tended by Leto and Artemis. But to deceive Diomedes and the others, Apollo fashions a double of Aeneas, a phantom or image (εἴδωλον), around which then the Trojans and Achaens continue their fight. Phoebus Apollo goes off, finally, to speak to Ares, pleading with him to enter the field and take from the battle this man Diomedes, who not only had rushed upon Apollo like a god (δαίμονι ἶσος), but who would fight even against father Zeus.

Let me first underline in the story Apollo's productive deed, his fashioning of an image of Aeneas, an image that appears so like Aeneas that both Trojans and Achaens, deceived by the illusion, continue the fighting. An appearing, illusory image, produced by the shining Apollo.

Around a second focal point let me assemble a series of epithets: according to the story just related Apollo is far-shooting or far-throwing (ἑκατηβόλος);[12] the *Homeric Hymn to Apollo* speaks of him as one who works from a distance (ἑκάεργος);[13] and at the beginning of *The Iliad* he is spoken of as far-darting (ἑκηβόλος).[14] Thus he is a god of distance, one set upon preserving the distance

10. *Iliad* V 431–59. Translation by Robert Fitzgerald (Garden City: Anchor, 1975).
11. Ibid., V 440–42.
12. Ibid., V 444. Forms of this epithet occur in other passages, e.g., I 75.
13. *Hymn to Apollo* 357, 382, etc.
14. *Iliad* I 14, 21, etc.

between sky and earth, between immortal god and mortal man, one ready to denounce any man who, like Diomedes, fails to observe the measure prescribed by this distance. Apollo's cry forces Diomedes back, denounces his god-like charge, reasserts the distance between the immortals of the open sky and earth-faring men.

A third focus is broached by an attribution near the beginning of *The Iliad:* Apollo is said to have given to Calchus that art of divination (μαντοσύνη) in which Calchus surpasses all men, that art by which he could tell truly what has been, what is, and what will be.[15] Such visionary words minister to man in ways not unlike such deeds as that by which Apollo protects Aeneas, such deeds also as are bespoken in the epithet that speaks of Apollo as the healer ('Iηπαιήων).[16]

In Nietzsche's text these three foci are in play, broached by allusion to certain names and deeds of Apollo and, in turn, organizing Nietzsche's discourse on the Apollinian. Let me now outline that discourse at the level prior to the arrival of the artist upon the scene, that is, at the level of the Apollinian as an art-impulse or art-state of nature.

The discourse concerns primarily the image, toward which the proto-artistic Apollinian has a double orientation. The initial focus is established by the phrase *"der schöne Schein der Traumwelten"* (III 1: 22). Here as well as throughout *The Birth of Tragedy* the word *Schein* will need to be read in its full range of senses: shine, look, appearance, semblance, illusion. Or, rather, more precisely, it will need to be read in its full spread of sense, since clearly it is not here a matter of simply polysemy. Even the very briefest sketch of a phenomenological analysis could indicate that it is a matter of senses so interlinked and mutually dependent that they form a field or spread rather than a series of distinct senses: in order for something to have a certain look, it must show itself, must shine forth; only insofar as it shines so as to have a look can it then become an appearance, for instance, an appearance *of* something else that perhaps does not shine forth; and only insofar as something has a certain look can it look *like* something else that it is not, hence become a semblance; finally, both appearance and semblance can develop into various modes of illusion, for instance, something can

15. Ibid., I 68–73.
16. *Hymn to Apollo* 272, 500, 517.

look so much like something else that it gives itself out as that other thing. Heidegger's analysis of phenomenon remains the paradigm of such analyses. [17] On the other hand, let it be clear that I do not propose to "apply" to Nietzsche's text either the Heideggerian analysis or another that would extend or modify that analysis. The reference to phenomenological analysis ought merely to call attention to the peculiar semantic spread so as to preclude restricting the sense in advance (for example, by simply translating *Schein* as *illusion*) and thus impoverishing in advance that very movement of Nietzsche's text that would both control and be controlled by the semantic spread. Let me, then, simply use the cognate form, not as a translation but in order to signal that the spread is in play.

Images shine. In dreams they shine forth as figures: "We delight in the immediate understanding of figure [*Gestalt*]; all forms [*Formen*] speak to us; there is nothing unimportant or superfluous" (III 1: 22). Dream images shine in such a way that one takes delight in them, an immediate delight in them simply as forms and figures. It is a beautiful shining, a shining of beautiful images, even when the images are not of things that could themselves be called beautiful, even when they are images of sad, gloomy things. One of the preliminary drafts, "The Dionysian Worldview," says of Apollo: "'Beauty' is his element" (III 2: 46). His element is not only the beauty of the shining dream image but also, in the broadest sense, the beautiful shining of the inner world of phantasy. Beauty is equally his element in the production of images, both of those belonging to the inner world of phantasy and of those fashioned in some material by another kind of phantasy. Apollo is "the god of all plastic powers [*bildnerische Kräfte*]" (III 1: 23).

But what is beauty? And how is it that shining can be beautiful? The same manuscript that identifies beauty as the god's element also poses the question with utter directness:

But what is beauty?—"The rose is beautiful" merely means: the rose has a good shine, it has something pleasantly radiant. Thereby nothing is to be asserted about its nature [*Wesen*]. It pleases, it arouses joy, as shine. (III 2: 65)

17. Heidegger, *Sein und Zeit* (1927; 9th ed., Tübingen: Max Niemeyer Verlag, 1960), §7A.

It is not as though the shining of an image may or may not be beautiful. Rather, the beautiful is determined precisely as shining, so that, whatever the image, to shine is to shine beautifully. It is to shine delightfully. This determination recalls that of the *Critique of Judgment:* the beautiful is that which delights merely by its sensible form without any regard to its actuality or its concept. [18] It recalls also the Platonic determination: the beautiful as τὸ ἐκφανέστατον. [19]

And yet, what of the ugly? For all is not simply beautiful. What of the rose when it is no longer beautiful, when it has wilted and begun to decay? What, for example, of obscene beasts and corpses? How is it that one takes delight in images of things that are themselves not in the least delightful? The question is a classical one, and it has a classical answer, one that invokes the distance of image from original, the spacing of mimesis. Aristotle is most explicit:

And it is also natural for all to delight in works of imitation [μίμησις]. This is shown by experience: though the objects themselves may be painful to see, we take delight in seeing the most perfect images [εἰκόνας] of them, for example, the forms of obscene beasts and of corpses. The reason is this. Learning [μανθάνειν] things gives great pleasure not only to philosophers but also to the rest of mankind, however small their capacity for it. The reason why we enjoy seeing images is that one is at the same time learning and gathering what each thing is. [20]

The delight requires the distance of image from original; and yet, what produces the delight is, according to Aristotle, the disclosiveness of the image, a disclosiveness that, operating across the distance, reveals the original (so that one is learning and gathering what each thing is) and yet, as a shining at a distance, leaves withdrawn what would be painful to see. Though the Apollinian may not be simply assimilable to the Aristotelian schema, it does retain the principal moments of that schema. The

18. Immanuel Kant, *Kritik der Urteilskraft* in *Kants Werke: Akademie-Textausgabe* (Berlin: Walter de Gruyter, 1968), especially VII (Einleitung) and § 5.
19. Plato, *Phaedrus* 250 d–e.
20. Aristotle, *Poetics* 1448 b.

delightful, beautiful, shining (the three words are rigorously tautological) is a disclosive shining at a distance.

This distance does not simply cancel the phantastic absorption in the images produced in the Apollinian state: Nietzsche insists that the images of the Apollinian dream world are not like mere shadows, since one is absorbed by them, living engagedly through the scenes. And yet, there is a peculiar feature of Apollinian shining that serves to limit such absorption, that announces the distance in such a way as, in turn, to provide one with a certain distance from the images, to render one's engagement contemplative, distanced. This feature Nietzsche describes as *"die durchschimmernde Empfindung ihres Scheins"* (III 1: 22). Always there glimmers the sensation that the dream image is shine—that is, the image shines forth in such a way as to betray in a fleeting sensation (*flüchtige Empfindung*) that it is just show, appearance, semblance. In the shining of the dream image there is a shimmering which fleetingly and delicately betrays that the image is image, not "original." Because of this shimmering betrayal, because the image appears *as* image, one is not engaged by it as though it were "original," as though it had the pressing reality of the things of everyday life. Contemplative distance is thus installed within the Apollinian state.

To the Apollinian there belongs, then, a delicate line (*zarte Linie*) demarcating the distance to be maintained from the image, a line generated by that fleeting sensation of shine that belongs to the shining of the image. The line is not to be overstepped; or, rather, it could be crossed only at the cost of violating the very character of the shining. Set at the distance thus marked, the distance of contemplation, one is free of the wilder emotions, one is calmly self-possessed. The Apollinian state is thus characterized by a certain measured or moderate delimitation (*maassvolle Begrenzung*), a delimitation that institutes both measure as well as the moderation that consists in fitting oneself to that measure. To accommodate oneself to a measure requires self-knowledge:

Apollo, as ethical deity, demands measure of his disciples, and, to be able to maintain it, self-knowledge. And so, alongside the aesthetic necessity of beauty, there occur the demands "know thyself" and "nothing in excess." (III 1: 24)

Apollo requires that one restrain oneself within the measure, the delimitation, of one's self. Apollo is "the glorious divine image of the *principium individuationis*" (III 1: 24).

And yet, the fleetingly self-betraying shining of Apollinian images not only generates a demand for knowledge but also is itself disclosive; as in the Aristotelian schema, the delight that one takes in the image is linked to its disclosiveness. Apollinian images offer a certain interpretation of life, bespeak a certain truth not commonly available. Such interpretation, such truth, passes beyond the image toward an original. Though, indeed, the Apollinian image shines in such a way as to betray that it is image and not original, it is, nonetheless, linked to an original, is an image *of* an original; one dreams always *of* something. Yet, within the Apollinian purview there is a curious inversion: it is the Apollinian image, not the imaged original, that is superior; and thus Nietzsche can write of "the higher truth, the perfection of these states in contrast to the incompletely intelligible everyday reality, the deep consciousness of nature, helping and healing in sleep and dreams" (III 1: 23). In Apollinian images the everyday originals, the things of the everyday, are perfected—that is, in the Apollinian state there is a gleam of perfection, of higher truth.[21] It is a perfection, a truth, whose shining provides a certain release from the negativity of the everyday, a certain relief from that fragmentariness, a healing.

It would be possible to double Nietzsche's discourse on the Apollinian, to double it with a discourse on imagination, extending what is broached by Nietzsche's reference to phantasy. Such a discourse would need to address the relation between imagination and truth, that higher truth that would be disclosed in the shining images that the Apollinian imagination would bring forth and with which it would be disclosively engaged. Such a discourse in and beyond the margin of *The Birth of Tragedy* would need to develop such questions as: What must be the constitution

21. In the manuscript "The Dionysian Worldview" (1870) Nietzsche is even more direct in linking Apollo to truth: "The god of beautiful shining must be at the same time the god of true knowledge" (III 2: 46). The fact that this formulation is not retained in *The Birth of Tragedy* is perhaps related to the significance that the opposition between theoretical and artistic comes to have in the published text, knowledge—though not truth—being set thus in opposition to art.

of imagination if it has the capacity to engage images that are disclosive of a higher truth? Does it suffice to term it *phantasy?* How, then, would one need to reformulate the distinction between imagination and phantasy, a distinction that in constantly varying forms runs throughout the entire history of metaphysics? Furthermore, if, in its productive engagement with shining images, imagination effects a disclosure of truth, then what must be the character of disclosure and of truth that they can be so linked to imagination? How extensive is Apollinian imagination? Do all other forms simply produce illusion or are there other forms that bear upon truth? Is there a Dionysian imagination, a form of imagination that comes into play in tragedy? Need it be said: the development of these questions could not but eventually be reflected back upon Nietzsche's text, reorienting and supplementing it.

Yet, even stopping short of this other discourse, one can discern in the Apollinian inversion, in its engagement with images disclosive of a higher truth, an eroding of that classical concept of mimesis that would determine the image as a falling away from the original, as impoverished by its distance from the original. To such a "false concept of mimesis," as it is termed in a note written in 1871, Nietzsche opposes another according to which "the artistic forms are more real than actuality, actuality is the imitation of the artistic forms." In the opposition it is a question of whether "the waking world is an imitation of the dreamworld" (III 3: 335).

Insofar as perfection is accorded to the image rather than to the original, the Apollinian inverts, in advance of Platonism, the order of origination that Platonism will bequeath to the history of metaphysics. Hence that notebook entry cited by Heidegger, to which I referred at the outset: "My philosophy an *inverted Platonism:* the further removed from true being, the purer, the more beautiful, the better it is. Living in shine as goal" (III 3: 207). And yet, in opposing to the everyday a more perfect sphere that would be more representational than simply presentational, the Apollinian turns, in advance, in the same direction as Platonism. A certain solidarity remains even if what is opposed to the everyday is what is called *idea.* This is a turn by which Plato is said to have expressed something deeply rooted in the Hellenic character: "the Platonic differentiation and evaluation of the 'idea' in opposition to the 'idol,' the copy, is deeply rooted in the Hellenic character" (III 1: 67–68). In the 1870 lectures on *Oedipus Tyrannos* Nietzsche is still more incisive regarding this point:

Nobler Greek antiquity had, not conceptually but instinctively, the same belief in the idea that later with Plato became conceptual. The individual was little developed, but the stem [*Stamm*], the race [*Geschlecht*], the state was the universal, the true being." (W 17: 295)

To the extent of this solidarity, Nietzsche does not simply think the Apollinian in symmetrical opposition to, as mere inversion of, Platonism. Nonetheless, what the Apollinian opposes to the everyday is the image, not the idea, and this opposition, this evaluation of the image-world over everyday actuality Nietzsche attributes to Plato the artist. Thus in a note from 1870–71: "That the world of representations is more real than actuality is a belief that Plato, as an *artistic nature* [*als Kunstlernatur*], set up theoretically" (III 3:114). By stopping the turn short of the Platonic order of origination, Nietzsche would rescue Plato the artist from the Platonic fable of the true world, that is, from the history of metaphysics.

Schopenhauer too had sought to rescue Plato the artist, even if only to submit Plato more inescapably to the modern, that is, Kantian, version of the fable. Indeed, the multiple cross-purposes that link *The Birth of Tragedy* to Schopenhauer's thought come into play almost from the moment that Schopenhauer is called upon, in the opening section, to lend his words to the discussion of the Apollinian. The parallel is drawn between, on the one hand, the Kantian distinction reconstituted by Schopenhauer as that between will and representation; and, on the other hand, the relation broached in the opening of Nietzsche's text between life and image. The parallel will have a certain linguistic enforcement, for Nietzsche will eventually describe the dream as a doubling of shine, as shine of shine (III 1: 35). And though, indeed, the language of shine is from the outset brought into play supporting the parallel, what first come peculiarly into question are the movements across the spaces delimited, respectively, by the parallel distinctions. Drawing the parallel between the aesthetically sensitive man's relation to dreams and, on the other side, the philosopher's relation to existence, Nietzsche then says in regard to the former: "from these images he interprets life for himself [*deutet er sich das Leben*]" (III 1: 23). The parallel would pre-scribe that, on the other side, the philosopher move interpretively from phenomena to thing-in-itself. And yet, thus virtually posing such an extension of the parallel, thus anticipating the parallel in-terpretive move on the side of the philosopher, Nietzsche *does not draw* the parallel, does not extend to the philosopher a parallel her-meneutical move from phenomena to thing-in-itself. Why not? No doubt because, in strict terms, the thing-in-itself is so utterly un-knowable that any such movement of interpretation would have to be declared illegitimate in principle. But why, then, anticipate the parallel only to forego drawing it? Presumably in order to mark Schopenhauer's duplicity in this regard. For what Nietzsche recog-nized almost from the time of his first encounter with Schopen-hauer's work was how readily and how frequently Schopenhauer crosses and recrosses the boundary, in principle uncrossable, be-tween phenomena and thing-in-itself. [22]

Another cross-purpose with Schopenhauer is more explicitly marked when Nietzsche proposes to apply to Apollo the words of Schopenhauer *in an eccentric sense* (*in einem excentrischen Sinne*). The words are, in part, already familiar, quoted directly from Schopenhauer:

"Just as on a stormy sea that, unbounded in all directions, raises and drops mountainous waves, howling, a sailor sits in a boat and trusts in his frail bark; so in the midst of a world of torments, the individual man sits quietly, supported by and trusting in the *principium individuationis.*" (III 1: 24)

The measured repose, the calm that comes of that self-knowledge by which Apollinian man accommodates himself to his indi-viduality—such is granted by the beautiful shining of Apollinian images. And yet, the purpose of Schopenhauer's words—before being reinscribed by Nietzsche—was not to describe the con-templative repose granted in the proto-artistic or artistic Apollinian state. Their purpose was, on the contrary, to describe something brought on only by a certain blindness, by the failure to see through the *principium individuationis:* the state of one enclosed

22. In this regard the most important text is Nietzsche's "Fragment einer Kritik der Schopenhauerischen Philosophie" (1867), M1: 392–401. This text will be discussed in chapter 2 (c) within the context of a more thorough differ-entiation between Schopenhauer and Nietzsche.

in his individuality by phenomena, by empirical existence, the state of one who has not yet reached the threshold of art.[23] It is not to one in such a state that Apollo is, as Nietzsche says, the most *sublime* expression of the repose of man wrapped in his individuality—sublime in that, by his very distance, by the way in which he exceeds earth-faring men, he draws them up into their repose. Shining from a distance, beautiful and sublime, Apollo is "the glorious divine image of the *principium individuationis*" (III 1: 24).

d

Now the artist arrives on the scene and enacts the transition from proto-artistic nature to art itself. Apollinian art arises as mimesis of proto-artistic nature, as imitation of that Apollinian impulse (of production) and state (of absorption) that bursts forth from nature prior to the advent of the human artist and without his mediation. Or, rather, such is the classical schema of mimesis that governs much of Nietzsche's analysis, that determines the very structure within which this classical schema will come eventually to be displaced.

In what way, then, is Apollinian art mimetic? How does it imitate nature? Three ways can be distinguished, or, rather, pieced together from the diverse indications given in Nietzsche's texts and notes from the early 1870s.

First, the creative impulse, the state in which the artist engages in creating the work of art, is imitative of the natural Apollinian state. It is akin to dreaming, a kind of play with the dream,[24] another production of images. In "The Dionysian Worldview" Nietzsche even describes the activity of the Apollinian artist, his actual creating of the work of art, as though it were only a kind of detour (*Umweg*) by which to lead others around to that dreamlike vision that he already enjoyed. Thus, the sculptor would shape the marble in order that one beholding it might come to see those forms—for instance, of the gods—

23. See the context in which the passage cited by Nietzsche occurs in Schopenhauer, WWV 1: §63.

24. "Thus, while the dream is the play of the individual man with what is actual, the art of the sculptor (in the broader sense) is his play with the dream" (III 2: 46).

that already hovered before his own phantastic vision. The epic poet would do much the same, though more indirectly, by leading the listener to engage himself in a certain artistic composing by which he would come to see the very figure or image that had hovered before the poet. The epic poet would have reached his goal "when he communicated to us that dreamlike condition in which he himself first produced that representation" (III 2: 55–56). To understand the epic storyteller is to call up the poetic image in one's own phantasy; as one of the notebook entries expresses it:

Now I assist [*nachhelfen*] with the phantasy, bring everything together, and have an image. Thus is the goal attained: I understand the image because I have myself produced it. (III 3: 53)

There is a mimetic relationship not only between the artistic state and the dream state but also between the images brought forth in these respective states. The images produced by Apollinian art shine like dream images, and one takes contemplative delight in that shining forth of a certain perfection, a higher truth. Apollinian art recreates and perfects the images of the proto-artistic natural state; and if "it was in dreams"—Nietzsche refers to Lucretius's view—"that the glorious figures of the gods first appeared to the souls of men" (III 1: 22), it is in Apollinian art that these figures are recreated and perfected into the Olympian world.

Nietzsche introduces an image, that of the artistic edifice (*Gebäude*) of Apollinian culture; this edifice, he says, must be levelled stone by stone if Apollinian art and what lies beneath it are to be exposed. The image is itself manifoldly Apollinian: simply as an image, as an image taken from an art that is in general Apollinian, and, as the ensuing description shows, as an image of such an artwork as was produced specifically by Greek Apollinian culture. The Greek temple with which Nietzsche begins will be razed; or, rather, as the Apollinian and its underground come to be exposed, it will be magically transformed.

Nietzsche describes the edifice:

First of all we see the glorious figures of the Olympian gods, standing on the gables of this structure. Their deeds, represented in brilliant reliefs, adorn its friezes. We must not be misled by the fact that Apollo stands side by side with the others as an individual deity, without any claim to priority of rank. The same impulse that embodied itself [*sich . . . versinnlichte*] in Apollo gave birth to this entire Olympian world, and in this sense Apollo is its father. (III 1: 30)

In Apollinian art there is operative, then, a linking of certain images that belong to different orders. Apollo is the artistic image of the artistic and proto-artistic Apollinian impulse; as such he is the image of the very impulse that gave rise not only to the other Olympian gods but also to himself. It is as (image of) this impulse that Apollo is the father of the entire Olympian world. The images of Apollo and of the other gods are, in turn, linked with still another order, with those images actually created in marble or adumbrated in words by the Apollinian artist. The statue is an image of the god, perhaps (as the manuscript and note discussed above suggest) in service to another vision, as a detour to its repetition. And yet, sculpture and epic poetry could hardly be just assimilated to the dreamlike vision in which one would simply, if phantastically, behold the god, as though the god were an original figure outside the μῦθος and not to any degree produced by it, as though art did not figure in the birth of the gods.

There is a third way in which Apollinian art imitates nature: its images, preeminently those of the Olympian gods, are imitations of mundane life, images of the everyday. Yet, in relation to the everyday they—no less than their proto-artistic counterparts—represent a certain perfecting; they let a certain perfection shine forth in contrast to the imperfect, everyday originals thus imaged. Nietzsche celebrates such perfection and the enhancement of life that it bespeaks:

For there is nothing here that suggests asceticism, spirituality, or duty: here there speaks to us only an exuberant, triumphant life in which all things, whether good or evil, are deified. And so the spectator may stand quite bewildered before this phantastic superabundance [*vor diesem phantastischen Ueberschwang*] of life, asking himself by virtue of what magic potion these high-spirited men could have found life so enjoyable that, wherever they turned, their eyes beheld the smile of Helen, the ideal picture of their own existence, "hovering in sweet sensuality." (III 1: 30–31)

The Olympian gods, the images created in Apollinian art, serve as transfiguring mirrors (*verklärende Spiegel*) in which life is revealed in a higher glory. In this sphere of beauty the Greeks behold their mirror-images (*Spiegelbilder*), the Olympian gods, and they are up-lifted and transformed by this vision.[25] Apollo's images cast their reflection back upon the everyday, transforming and justifying it:

The same impulse that brings art to life as the completion and consum-mation of existence, seducing one to a continuation of life, also gives rise to the Olympian world, in which the Hellenic "will" holds up to itself a transfiguring mirror. Thus do the gods justify the life of man: they them-selves live it—the only satisfactory theodicy! Existence under the bright sunshine of such gods is regarded as desirable in itself. (III 1: 32)

The images produced by Apollinian art are in this sense superior to their originals; they are images in which the everyday shines forth in a higher truth or, rather, in which a higher truth comes to shine through and beyond the everyday.

And yet, it is not only a matter of transfiguring the dullness and incompleteness of everyday life. Something much more powerful, a more profound need, stands behind the creation of the beautiful world of the Olympians. Nietzsche finds expression of this need in what Greek folk wisdom had to say even in the face of exuberant life, in the profoundly pessimistic words that the captured Silenus is said to have addressed to all men through King Midas, that "what is best of all is utterly beyond your reach: not to be born, not to *be,* to be *nothing,*" that "the second best for you is—to die soon" (III 1: 31).[26] This is the wisdom that underlies the creation of the Olympian gods, that drives the Greeks to create them. Now the image of the artistic edifice, of the temple with its brilliant reliefs and adorned friezes, is transformed, as if magically:

Now the Olympian magic mountain [*Zauberberg*], as it were, opens before us and reveals its roots to us. The Greek knew and felt the terrors and horrors [*Schrecken und Entsetzlichkeit*] of existence. In order to be able to live at all, he had to set up before them the radiant dream birth of the Olympians. . . . In order to be able to live, the Greeks had to create these gods from a most profound need. (III 1: 31–32)

25. A note from 1870–71 reads: "Greek mythology deified *all* the forms of significant humanity" (III 3: 104).

26. In *Oedipus at Colonus* (1224–26) the chorus says:

Not to be born surpasses thought and speech.
The second best is to have seen the light
And then to go back quickly whence we came.

Apollinian art not only serves to reveal life in those transfiguring mirrors, the Olympian gods, in which it shines forth "surrounded with a higher glory" (III 1: 32); it serves also to veil life, to veil the terrors and horrors of the existential underground, to veil and withdraw from sight that the very vision of which would otherwise incapacitate life and provoke its negation. Indeed, as a note from 1869–70 says, "The world of the Greek gods is a fluttering veil, which covers [verhüllte] what is most frightful" (III 3: 77). And in the words of another note, "There are no beautiful surfaces without a terrible depth" (III 3: 167).[27] Apollinian art serves to veil what will prove to be most appropriately called not even just terrible depth but abyss.

Nietzsche calls it the Dionysian. And so, along with the mimetic order that I have attempted to reconstruct as such, there is also a historical order. Nietzsche is explicit about it from the beginning: the Apollinian can never have been a simple condition, an arcadian harmony of the naive artist with nature. As Nietzsche writes in a letter to Rohde a few months after the publication of *The Birth of Tragedy*, "this world of purity and beauty did not drop from the sky" (BKG II 3: 23); rather, it arose only through an overthrowing of Titans and a slaying of monsters (III 1: 33). The Apollinian must always already have been incited by the Dionysian. Hence, Nietzsche orders Greek history by an ordering of the development of Greek art through the antagonism of the two art impulses: the reign of the folk wisdom voiced by Silenus was overcome through the Homeric world to which the Apollinian impulse gave rise;[28] the latter, overwhelmed by the influx of the Dionysian, again arose in the austerity of Doric art; until finally a mysterious

27. The same statement occurs in the discarded draft of the "Foreword to Richard Wagner": "Greek art has taught us that there are no beautiful surfaces without a terrible depth" (III 3: 368).

28. In "Homer's Contest" Nietzsche writes of the pre-Homeric world that incited and was, in turn, overcome by Apollinian art: "But what lies, as the womb of everything Hellenic, *behind* the Homeric world? . . . Where do we look, if, no longer guided and protected by Homer's hand, we step backwards into the pre-Homeric world? Only into night and horror, into the products of a phantasy accustomed to the horrible. What earthly existence is reflected in the loathsome-awful theogonian lore: a life swayed only by the *children of the night,* strife, amorous desires, deception, age, and death" (III 2: 278–79).

marriage bond (*geheimnissvolles Ehebündniss*) was established between the antagonists. The history ends with the birth of tragedy.

Nietzsche ventures also to sketch a third order, an order that one could be tempted to call metaphysical, since it is posed by way of the Schopenhauerian reconstitution of the metaphysical distinction between phenomenon and thing-in-itself. In effect, the order is composed simply by joining the two relations that in the initial reference to Schopenhauer were presented merely as parallel: the thing-in-itself, now characterized (not without reservation) as "the truly existent primal one, eternally suffering and contradictory [*das Wahrhaft-Seiende und Ur-Eine, als das ewig Leidende und Widerspruchsvolle*] (III 1: 34), shines forth as empirical reality (as phenomena, determined by space, time, and causality); and the latter, in turn, shines forth in the dream. Thus bringing the language of shine fully into play, Nietzsche adds that the primal one needs the double shining for its redemption (*Erlösung*). But the additional connection is not asserted without reservation: Nietzsche calls it a "metaphysical assumption" to which he feels himself impelled.

Before finally turning to Apollo so as to draw within the new order the reference to him as the sublime expression of the *principium individuationis* and of the redemption of the primal one, Nietzsche introduces a new image. The Apollinian is no longer a Greek temple or a magic mountain but has now become a painting by Raphael. In Raphael's "Transfiguration," the upper and lower halves of the painting, respectively, are the "Apollinian world of beauty and its substratum, the terrible wisdom of Silenus" (III 1: 35). In the painting, an Apollinian artwork, he painted both Apollinian and Dionysian and thus in a sense brought painting as close as possible to that union of the two art worlds that is achieved in tragedy.

But what about the metaphysical order that would be parallel to the two worlds painted by Raphael? And what about redemption in shine? It is too soon to attempt to draw the limits of Nietzsche's appropriation of Schopenhauer's metaphysics; that there are rather narrow limits is evident from the cross-purposes that have already come to light, but their precise determination must await discussion of the Dionysian. For now let it suffice to note a common identification of the existential substratum and then to trace the directions that, for Schopenhauer and Nietzsche, respectively, redemption in shine would take; it will be important to mark the divergence between these directions.

It is remarkable how literally Schopenhauer expresses those words of pessimistic wisdom that Nietzsche puts in the mouth of Dionysus's companion Silenus. In the metaphysical order the pessimism derives from the thing-in-itself, which is redetermined by Schopenhauer as will; what resounds throughout that order is only the aimless unsatisfiable striving of a will at variance with itself (WWV 1: §§27, 56). Thus, everywhere among the phenomena in which the will appears, there is contest, struggle, universal conflict, a never-ending war of extermination between individuals (WWV 1: §§27, 28). Not only are human endeavors and desires fated to repeat perpetually the dull round of satisfaction transformed into new desire, of pleasure dissolved into pain (WWV 1: §29), but also, in Schopenhauer's words, if "we were to bring to the sight of everyone the terrible sufferings and afflictions to which his life is constantly exposed, he would be seized with horror." Hence, "the shortness of life, so often lamented, may perhaps be the very best thing about it" (WWV 1: §59). Or, at least, as Silenus would have it: "the second best for you is—to die soon." And, indeed, more than once Schopenhauer quotes the words of Calderón (WWV 1: §§51, 63):

> For man's greatest offence
> Is that he has been born.

Silenus again: "What is best of all is utterly beyond your reach: not to be born, not to *be,* to be *nothing.*" Schopenhauer would even find in tragedy, as its true sense, the insight that the hero must atone not just for his own particular sins but for the guilt of existence itself, for the offence of having been born (WWV 1: §51).

But what, then, of redemption? How is redemption possible? Does the will find salvation through its shining forth as phenomena? Though considered in itself it may be only blind, irresistible urge (*Drang*), the addition of the phenomenal world gives the will only a mirror for itself, not deliverance from itself. And even if, in the end, it is knowledge that leads to salvation, that knowledge is of a kind constituted far beyond the level of mere phenomenal appearances. What the will beholds of itself in the mirror of phenomena is only the phenomenal transcription of the pessimistic wisdom of Silenus, an image of the sufferings and afflictions of life.

Redemption is brought by art, redemption both from the everyday (phenomenal) world and from the deeper world that would underlie it. On this point there is complete solidarity between Schopenhauer and Nietzsche. Furthermore, it is a matter of contemplation that would provide deliverance from the boundless striving of the will:

Then all at once the peace, always sought but always escaping us on that first path of willing, comes to us of its own accord, and all is well with us. . . . This liberation of knowledge lifts us as wholly and completely above all this as do sleep and dreams. (WWV 1: §38)

Such contemplation is, Schopenhauer adds, "the only pure happiness that is not preceded either by suffering or need, or yet followed by repentance, suffering, emptiness, or satiety" (WWV 1: §58)—in short, contemplative deliverance from all that is frightful and terrible.

And yet, for Schopenhauer the contemplation brought by art is a contemplation of ideas, which can become objects of knowledge only by the abolition of individuality in the knowing subject; such contemplation is, then, a matter of losing oneself in the object, forgetting one's individuality, coming to exist not as will but as pure subject mirroring the ideas (WWV 1: §§30, 34). At the summit of art such contemplative knowledge becomes a quieter of all willing, producing resignation, self-abolition of the will, hence redemption (*Erlösung*) (WWV 1: §48).

The divergence could hardly be more striking. For Nietzsche's Apollinian artist what are to be contemplated are images, not ideas. The difference is decisive, even if Schopenhauer's efforts to distinguish ideas from abstract concepts and his insistence on the perceptual nature of the ideas serve to reduce somewhat the extent of the difference.[29] It is decisive because Nietzsche's Apollinian is

29. Schopenhauer understands ideas in what he takes to be the Platonic sense: as patterns, as the eternal forms of things. Adapted to his metaphysics of the will, ideas are thus determined as the different "grades of the objectivity of the will" (WWV 1: §25); or as "the most adequate objectivity possible of the will" (WWV 1: §32). Schopenhauer insists on the difference between ideas, thus determined, and abstract concepts: "The *concept* [Begriff] is abstract, discursive, wholly undetermined within its sphere, determined only by its limits, attainable and intelligible only to him who has the faculty of reason, communicable by words

precisely the affirmation, intensification, perfection, of individuality, not its abolition. If one is to discover a *positive* relation of Apollinian images to the Silenic underground (comparable to the character of Schopenhauer's ideas as grades of the objectivity of the will), if one is to discover in Nietzsche's analysis a capacity of art to disrupt the limits of individuality, one must look beyond Apollinian art toward tragedy. But even in tragedy it will never be, for Nietzsche, a matter of resignation from life but rather of life's justification and transfiguration.

Near the end of *The Birth of Tragedy* Nietzsche describes the mimetic relation of art to nature as that of a supplement. The passage is one to which it will be necessary to return at virtually every stage of the reading of *The Birth of Tragedy:*

. . . art is not merely imitation of the reality of nature [*Nachahmung der Naturwirklichkeit*] but rather a metaphysical supplement of the reality of nature, placed beside it for its overcoming. (III 1: 147)

Art is indeed imitation of nature, yet not merely such, not merely a mimetic double, a fabricated image, that would leave its original simply intact and unaffected. Let it suffice at this stage to have observed how Apollinian art places its images, especially the figures of the Olympian gods, Apollo's images, beside the reality of nature in such a way as to overcome the negativity of the everyday through the vision of exuberant life; but also how, by the very brilliance with which those images shine, such art veils the incomparably more threatening negativity of what will be called the abyss. It could also be called the boundless, *das Masslose.*

---

without further assistance, entirely exhausted by its definition. The *idea* [Idee] on the other hand, definable perhaps as the adequate representative [*Repräsentant*] of the concept, is absolutely perceptive, and, although representing [*vertretend*] an infinite number of individual things, is yet thoroughly definite" (WWV 1: §49). Yet, he also insists on another distinction that would seem once for all to preclude reducing the difference between the idea and the Apollinian image: "for the idea is not really the spatial figure hovering before me [*die mir vorschwebende räumliche Gestalt*], but its expression, its pure significance, its innermost essence, disclosing itself and appealing to me; and it can be wholly the same in spite of great difference in the spatial relations of the figure" (WWV 1: §41). One can only be astounded that Schopenhauer does not bring to bear on these differentiations the resources of Kant's theory of schematism.

| # D I O N Y S U S —

Resounding Excess

The figure of Dionysus is different. It is a figure drawn, or rather withdrawn, in such a manner that it can have no direct image, even though, on the other hand, it can become in its way directly manifest, to say nothing quite yet of the appearance of Dionysus on the stage of Greek tragedy. This figure could be considered the most perfectly metaphysical, the original *an sich,* so compactly an original, so thoroughly *an sich,* as to withhold itself from direct disclosure in an image. And yet, by virtue of this very withdrawing, it can also be considered an excessive figure, one that exceeds the circuit of metaphysics, a figure in excess of metaphysics, resounding from beyond closure, ἐπέκεινα τῆς οὐσίας. The figure is itself a figure of excess, a disfiguring of difference, its release from the constraints within which metaphysics would control it. One could call it difference itself, difference as such, were not its release the very disruption of the limits that would determine the *itself* and the *as such.* One could call it also *das Masslose*—that is, abyss. Yet not without also submitting the discourse to an abysmal effect, a doubling that crosses what is said with an unsaying, that spaces the discourse.

a

Nonetheless, it is on the stage that Dionysus shines forth most brilliantly. It is in Greek tragedy, above all, that the figure of Dionysus is inscribed. Indeed, virtually the entire force of Nietzsche's text is brought into play to demonstrate at the core of Greek tragedy a manifestation of the Dionysian—to such an extent that Nietzsche can proclaim all the heroes of Greek tragedy (Prometheus, Oedipus, etc.) to be, in the end, merely masks of Dionysus. The hermeneutics of Nietzsche's text is such as to engage that text with Greek tragedy from the beginning: it is preeminently Greek tragedy that makes manifest the figure of Dionysus, through which, in turn, a certain understanding of tragedy as such is to be gained, following that understanding of art embodied in such figures by the Greeks.

Among the surviving Greek tragedies there is only one that is explicitly about Dionysus; this drama, *The Bacchae,* is indispensable for recovering the figure of the god, and indeed Nietzsche's text has several important references to it. Not that Dionysus is simply and directly represented in this drama: not only does the dark background hymned by the chorus permeate the entire drama, but also, even on the stage, there is still a certain play of masks by which, as Nietzsche says in general, "the god who appears speaks and acts so as to resemble an erring, striving, suffering individual" (III 1: 68). Yet, in *The Bacchae* this difference is posed most transparently, and the very movement of the play is toward its utter effacement, toward the revelation that the Bacchic Stranger is none other than Dionysus himself. [1]

One might also say that in *The Bacchae* Dionysus is most powerfully manifest. For granted that throughout his career Euripides was set on driving Dionysus out of tragedy, reconstituting it on an essentially non-Dionysian basis, *The Bacchae* represents the moment when the god can no longer be excluded, the moment when Euripides is finally driven to glorify his adversary, the moment of the return of the repressed in all its power (see III 1: 78). A kind of palinode, Nietzsche calls it in the lectures on *Oedipus Tyrannos* in-

---

1. In this connection Jean-Pierre Vernant stresses the function of the mask: "The mask worn by the god and the human stranger—who is also the god—is the tragic mask of the actor, the function of which is to make the characters recognizable as what they are, to render them visually identifiable. But in the case of Dionysus, the mask disguises him as much as it proclaims his identity; it literally 'masks' him; at the same time, through his misidentification and secret, this prepares the way for his authentic triumph and revelation. All the characters in the drama, including the chorus composed of his faithful female Lydian devotees, who have followed him to Thebes, see only the foreign missionary in the theatrical mask that the god wears. The spectators also see that foreigner but realize that he is a disguise for the god, a disguise through which the latter can eventually be made known for what he is: a masked god whose coming will bring the fulfillment of joy to some, but to others, those unable to recognize him, nothing but destruction. The ambiguity of the mask worn by the stranger and by the god expresses the interplay between the two" (Jean-Pierre Vernant and Pierre Vidal-Naquet, *Myth and Tragedy in Ancient Greece* [New York: Zone Books, 1988], 382).

asmuch as Euripides "lets himself be torn to pieces as Pentheus, the reasonable, rationalistic opponent of the Dionysian cult" (W 17: 299; cf. W 18: 49).

In *The Bacchae*[2] the manifestation of Dionysus is both sung by the chorus and enacted on stage. The drama opens with Dionysus's assertion of his identity; alone on stage, disguised as the exotic, foreign leader of a band of devotees of Dionysus, he begins the opening soliloquy:

> I am Dionysus, the son of Zeus,
> Come back to Thebes, this land where I was born.
> My mother was Cadmus's daughter, Semele by name,
> Midwived by fire, delivered by the lightning's
> Blast.
>
> (B 1–3)

It is this identity that Dionysus has made manifest by teaching his dances and by establishing his mysteries and rites:

> That I might be revealed on earth for what I am:
> A god.
>
> (B 22)

It is also this identity that is dramatically contested in *The Bacchae*.[3] First of all, against his mother's sisters, who slander him by saying that in truth he was fathered by a man, Semele fathering off her shame on Zeus, who in anger then blasted her with lightning. When the play opens, Dionysus has already begun the

---

2. Use has been made of the translation of *The Bacchae* by William Arrowsmith in *Greek Tragedies,* ed. David Grene and Richmond Lattimore (Chicago: University of Chicago Press, 1960), vol. 3; and of the translation by G. S. Kirk, *The Bacchae of Euripides* (Cambridge: Cambridge University Press, 1979); along with the Greek text and commentary given in Dodds's edition: E. R. Dodds, ed., *Bacchae* (Oxford: Oxford University Press, 1960).

3. Vernant writes: "The Dionysus of the *Bacchae* is a god intent upon imposing his imperious, demanding, overwhelming presence upon this earthly world: He is a god of *'parousia'*. In every land, every city that he decides to make his own, he makes his entrance, arrives, is there. The very first word of the play is ἥκω: 'Here I am, I have come.' Dionysus always bursts in suddenly, as if erupting from somewhere else, somewhere foreign, a barbarian world, far away. . . . The entire tragedy, as it unfolds showing us the Dionysiac epiphany, illustrates this 'coming' " (Vernant and Vidal-Naquet, *Myth and Tragedy,* 390).

contest, the manifestation, by stinging all the women of Thebes with frenzy and driving them up to the mountains where they wander in madness. Pentheus, too, the young king who denies the identity of Dionysus, will be brought to recognize the god:

> Therefore I shall show myself to be god, to him
> And to all the Thebans.

(B 47–48)

Indeed, the drama centers on the manifestation of the identity of the god to Pentheus, a manifestation that culminates in a Dionysian destruction of Pentheus, one in which Pentheus undergoes the very destruction characteristic of Dionysus himself and reenacted by his followers. Especially at the moment when the messenger tells how Pentheus was torn to pieces by the Maenads, the young king, first cousin of Dionysus, becomes an image, a mask, of Dionysus himself. Thus he is driven not merely to recognize the identity of the god but to embody, to enact, that identity to the point of his own destruction.

As the drama moves toward that moment of Dionysian truth, it plays out in various ways the manifestation of the identity of the god; most notably, perhaps, in the various doublings that serve dramatically to contest that identity and, in contesting it, to make it manifest. From the beginning, in the opening words of the disguised Dionysus, there is the question of his double origin, the question posed by Semele's sisters: whether he is the son not just of a mortal but also of a god. In the opening hymn the chorus then sings of his double birth, of his having been born twice, delivered of his mother by the lightning that consumed her, then bound in the thigh of Zeus, concealed from Hera, protected as in a second womb from which he was to be delivered when the time was fulfilled (B 88–104). And yet, the old Teiresias contests the story, retells it as a story of another doubling: from a fragment of ether Zeus is said to have molded a dummy of Dionysus and to have given it to Hera as a hostage. A pun is made to account for the transformation of this story into the one commonly told: the story was made by changing the word *hostage* (ὅμηρος)—or, rather the verbal form (ὡμήρευσε) into the word *thigh* (μηρός) (286–97). Later, when Dionysus tells of Pentheus's futile efforts to bind him in the stable, it is again a matter of doubling: in his delusion Pentheus

45

sets about trying to rope the knees and hooves of a bull, while the bull-horned god Dionysus

> sat nearby,
> Quietly watching.
>
> (B 621–22)

Then rushing in alarm to the palace, drawing his sword, Pentheus again is deluded by a double, a phantom:

> There, it seems,
> Bromius had made a shape, a phantom which resembled me,
> Within the court. Bursting in, Pentheus thrust and stabbed
> At that thing of gleaming air as though he thought it me.
>
> (B 629–31)

Pentheus is deluded not only about the identity of Dionysus but equally about his own identity. When, before the scene in the stable, he orders Dionysus chained and proclaims himself the stronger, Dionysus speaks to him directly:

> You do not know
> The limits of your strength. You do not know
> What you do. You do not know who you are.
>
> (B 506)

When Pentheus answers by citing his name and the names of his father and mother, Dionysus alludes to the pun connecting his name to *mourning* (πένθος) and hints at what is to befall Pentheus in his delusion:

> You are apt in your name for falling into misfortune.
>
> (B 508)

In being dismembered, Pentheus will not only suffer utter loss of identity but will be made to imitate, at the cost of his own destruction, the identity of the god whom he has blasphemed; at the moment of his horrible death, he will have become a double of the god.

All these doublings serve to make manifest the identity of Dionysus. They serve to show that the identity of the god is an identity to which doubling belongs, that it is a sundered identity, an identity to which belongs a difference that both recent scholars[4]

---

4. For example, Kirk, in his Introduction to his translation, *The Bacchae of Euripides*, 5.

and Nietzsche himself (III 1: 37) tend to call contradiction. It will be necessary to ask whether this difference, as manifested in *The Bacchae* and as thought in *The Birth of Tragedy,* can be sufficiently delimited by the concept of contradiction; or whether this concept does not already constrain it within the very system that it would exceed and disrupt, constituting thus only a metaphysical double of the Dionysian.

The double nature of Dionysus is mirrored in his followers. Stung with frenzy, the women of Thebes have been driven out of their homes into the open air, out of the city up to Mount Cithaeron, out of their wits in their service to the god, so much so as not even to recognize their own offspring, as will be shown in all its horror by the case of Agave, Pentheus's mother, who is first among those who tear him to pieces. And yet, along with such distraction, there is also contraction:

> There they sit,
> Rich and poor alike, even the daughters of Cadmus,
> Beneath the silver firs on the roofless rocks.

> (B 37–38)

In their madness there is community of rich and poor, even with the daughters of the founder of the city; there is also communion of the women with nature, with the earth, from which at their beckoning there springs water, wine, milk, and honey.[5]

The Maenads hold communion also with beasts of the earth:

> Breasts swollen with milk,
> New mothers who had left their babies behind at home
> Nestled gazelles and young wolves in their arms,
> Suckling them.

> (B 699–702)[6]

5. "Euripides seems to hint likewise at a further effect, a merging of the individual consciousness in a group consciousness: the worshipper θιασεύεται ψυχάν [has his soul imbued with Bacchic revelry] (*Ba.* 75), he is at one not only with the Master of Life but with his fellow-worshippers; and he is at one also with the life of earth (*Ba.* 726–7)" (Dodds, *Bacchae,* xx).

6. In "The Dionysian Worldview" Nietzsche refers explicitly to this passage (III 2: 51). A related text, "The Birth of the Tragic Conception," actually cites this passage in the course of citing a portion of the messenger's report on what was seen by those who went to Cithaeron to spy on the women (III 2: 79). There is also a reference in the lectures on *Oedipus Tyrannos:* "Some take gazelles and young wild wolves in their arms and suckle them" (W 17: 299).

Yet also, as if in utter contradiction, they fall upon the beasts and tear them to pieces. The messenger tells of how he and the other herdsmen barely escaped being torn to pieces by the women, who were seen to swoop down upon the herds of cattle:

> And then
> You could have seen a single woman with bare hands
> Tear a fat calf, still bellowing with fright,
> In two, while others clawed the heifers to pieces.
> There were ribs and cloven hooves scattered everywhere,
> And scraps smeared with blood hung from the fir trees.
>
> (B 737–42)

As Actaeon, Cadmus's grandson, is said to have been torn to pieces on Cithaeron by his own hounds. As Pentheus, too, will suffer dismemberment (σπαραγμός) at the hands of his own mother. As Dionysus himself was said to have been torn to pieces by the Titans. Nietzsche recalls this last story, linking it to the dual nature of the god, interpreting it as portraying the issue of individuation, which is to come to its end with the restoration of oneness that will be brought by the rebirth of Dionysus (III 1: 68).

Though in *The Birth of Tragedy* this story functions at several levels, what primarily comes to light in this connection in *The Bacchae* is the duality of (re)union and dismemberment, the duality that belongs to Dionysus, the difference that sunders his identity. The same duality is again made manifest in what is known to have been the culmination of the Dionysian mountain dance (ὀρειβασία): tearing an animal to pieces *and* eating the raw flesh (ὠμοφαγία).[7] In the words sung by the chorus in the epode that concludes the opening hymn of *The Bacchae:*

> Blood of the goat that is slain,
> Joy of the living flesh devoured.
>
> (B 138)

Dionysus's votaries tear to pieces only then to consume: the joy and rapture of reunion in the most intimate connection with the pain and terror of dismemberment.

At the point in the drama where Pentheus has gone off to be costumed in women's clothes and where Dionysus openly foretells

---

7. Dodds, *Bacchae,* xvi.

that the king will be killed by his own mother, there is a proclamation of the double nature of the god. The simplicity and transparency of Dionysus's proclamation is stunning:

> He shall come to know
> Dionysus, son of Zeus, consummate god,
> Most terrible [δεινότατος], and yet most gentle [ἠπιώτατος], to
> mankind.

(B 859–61)

The dual nature of the god is not only proclaimed but also sung in the choral hymn that immediately follows the proclamation. The strophe hymns that most gentle side:

> When shall I dance once more
> With bare feet the all-night dances,
> Tossing my head for joy
> In the damp air, in the dew,
> As a running fawn might frisk
> For the green joy of the wide fields.

(B 862–67)

The antistrophe sings of the other, the most terrible side:

> Slow but unmistakable
> The might of the gods moves on.
> It punishes that man,
> Infatuate of soul
> And hardened in his pride,
> Who disregards the gods.
> The gods are crafty:
> They lie in ambush
> A long step of time
> To hunt the unholy.

(B 882–90)

And yet, how is it that the two sides are of one and the same god? Where, within the difference, is the identity of Dionysus to be found? The identity has to do preeminently with bonds that would constrain one within certain limits. It has to do with the breaking of such bonds, as the bonds were broken that would otherwise have held those Bacchic women who were clapped in chains and sent to the dungeon by Pentheus:

49

> The chains on their legs snapped apart
> By themselves. Untouched by any human hand,
> The doors swung wide, opening of their own accord.
>
> (B 446–47)

Just as the chains could not bind Dionysus himself; just as he could not be held in prison. Whether it is a matter of the duality of dismemberment and reunion or of the duality of dismemberment and consumption, both sides of the duality bespeak a disruption of the limits that would delimit the individual, either effacing those limits by way of a reunion or consumption that would reunite the individual to what otherwise would be determinately other; or else cancelling by dismemberment the limits that otherwise would enclose the individual, tearing the individual to pieces. Both as most terrible and as most gentle, Dionysus breaks the bonds of individuation and all the constraints of family, city, and custom that are linked to the delimitation of the individual.[8]

b

In *The Birth of Tragedy* the Dionysian is to be outlined first as a natural art-state, as the other of those two "artistic energies that burst forth from nature itself *without the mediation of the human artist*" (III 1: 26). By way of initial orientation it is to be thought as the world of frenzy or intoxication (*Rausch*)—that is, its difference from the Apollinian is to be taken as analogous to the contrast between the two physiological phenomena, frenzy and dream.

The duality that *The Bacchae* makes manifest in the Dionysian is broached almost from the outset of *The Birth of Tragedy*. On the one side, Nietzsche writes:

8. A note from 1871 reads: "The Dionysian genius—has nothing to do with the state" (III 3: 334). Nietzsche elaborates in *The Birth of Tragedy:* "After all, in every case in which Dionysian excitement gains any significant extent one can always trace how the Dionysian liberation from the fetters of the individual finds expression first of all in a diminution of, in indifference to, indeed, in hostility to, the political instincts. Just as certainly, Apollo who forms states is also the genius of the *principium individuationis,* and state and patriotism cannot live without an affirmation of the individual personality" (III 1: 129). Nietzsche's concern in this context is to show how tragedy reinstalls Dionysian man in the political, making it possible that "the people of the tragic mysteries" are the very ones who "fight the battle against the Persians."

Under the magic of the Dionysian not only is the bond between man and man reestablished, but nature, which has become alienated, hostile, or subjugated, celebrates once more its reconciliation with its lost son, man. (III 1: 25)

Man is reunited not only with nature but also with man:

Now all the rigid, hostile barriers [*Abgrenzungen*] that necessity, caprice, or "impudent convention" have fixed between man and man are broken. Now . . . each one feels himself not only united, reconciled, fused with his neighbor, but as one with him. (III 1: 25)

Such joy of reunion of man with man and with nature belongs to the side of Dionysian nature that is most gentle.

But Dionysus is also most terrible, and along with the joy of reunion there is the genuinely Dionysian suffering of dismemberment: it is as if, says Nietzsche, nature "were heaving a sigh at her dismemberment into individuals" (III 1: 29, 68). Nietzsche is explicit about the duality: "Dionysus has the dual nature [*Doppelnatur*] of a cruel, barbarized demon and of a mild, gentle ruler" (III 1: 68). The same duality belongs to the votaries of Dionysus, those "dually-minded revelers [*zwiefach gestimmte Schwärmer*]." The duality is indeed what especially links the Dionysian Greek to the Dionysian barbarian:

Only the curious blending and duality in the emotions of the Dionysian revelers remind us—as medicines remind us of deadly poisons—of the phenomenon that pain begets joy, that jubilation may wring sounds of agony from us. (III 1: 29)

Note especially the reference to medicines and deadly poisons: even though the explicit sense of the passage is that, by the presence of the duality, the Dionysian Greek reminds one of the Dionysian barbarian as medicines remind one of deadly poisons, this duality of medicine/poison also itself exemplifies the Dionysian duality at issue here. The Dionysian duality is akin to that of the φάρμακον: reunion/dismemberment, healing/killing.[9]

---

9. In *The Bacchae* Teiresias uses the word φάρμακον in its double sense when he describes the madness of Pentheus, an inversion, as it were, of Dionysian μανία: "For you are mad, cruelly mad: no drug can cure your sickness but some drug has caused it" (B 326–27). See Dodds's commentary on these lines (*Bacchae*, 112).

In *The Birth of Tragedy* the identity to which the duality belongs, the identity of the Dionysian, is also explicit almost from the outset: for instance, at the point where Nietzsche says of the Dionysian that "it does not heed the singular but even seeks to annihilate the individual" (III 1: 26). It is indicated likewise in the initial discussion of the Dionysian where Nietzsche links the duality (terror/rapture, *Grausen/Verzückung*) to the collapse of the principle of individuation: the welling up of such terror and rapture at the collapse of the principle of individuation provides "a glimpse into the nature of the *Dionysian*" (III 1: 24). On both sides of the Dionysian—whether Dionysus be most terrible or most gentle, whether what arises in his revelers be terror or rapture—the effect is to disrupt the limit that would delimit the individual subject, to violate the *principium individuationis*.

Let it be said at once: everything will depend on how one interprets this disruption, which constitutes the identity of the Dionysian, even while, on the other hand, disrupting the very operation of the concept of identity, suspending it over an abyss. How one interprets this disruptive, abysmal identity will determine not only how tragedy is to be thought but also how it is to be (dis)placed in its opposition to that other possibility that Nietzsche calls Socratism but already begins to think as Platonism or metaphysics, as in the texts of the late 1880s in which he proclaims an end, an inversion and displacement. The turn that will be even more at issue a century later—as the end or closure of metaphysics—will never have been independent of the abyss with which thought is confronted by the Dionysian.

Everything will depend on a certain spacing, on setting the Dionysian and, hence, tragedy apart from metaphysics, on resisting their assimilation specifically to Schopenhauer's metaphysics, which, on the other hand, is indisputably reinscribed in Nietzsche's text. Everything will depend on sustaining a certain strategic resistance in the face of this reinscription. Otherwise *The Birth of Tragedy* will simply be assimilated in an all-too-familiar way to Schopenhauer's metaphysics, which belongs utterly to that metaphysics of which Nietzsche will tell in the story of "How the 'True World' Finally Became a Fable." A rigorous differentiation would then be authorized at least between *The Birth of Tragedy* and the texts of the late 1880s that announce the inversion and displacement of metaphysics.

But initially there are other resources for interpreting the identity of the Dionysian, resources that, provided they are developed apart from the reinscriptions of Schopenhauer's metaphysics, work against the assimilation and set Nietzsche's text sliding away from the metaphysical axis with which it could otherwise simply be aligned.

Among these resources is the following note, written in fall 1869, concerning the folk-impulses from which drama arose:

In those orgiastic festivals of Dionysus there prevailed such a degree of being-outside-oneself [Ausser-sich-sein], of ἔκστασις, that men acted and felt like transformed and enchanted beings. (III 3: 6)

This note is echoed in *The Birth of Tragedy* in a passage where Nietzsche refers to "the rapture [Verzückung] of the Dionysian state with its annihilation of the ordinary bounds and limits of existence" (III 1: 52). In another, very remarkable passage in the lecture "The Greek Music Drama," presented in 1870, he underlines and elaborates the link between drama, hence the Dionysian, and enchantment, ecstasy, being-outside-oneself. Here is his description of the mysterious sources of ancient drama:

The all-powerful, suddenly appearing effect of spring here augments also the life-forces to such excess [Übermass] that ecstatic states [ekstatische Zustände], visions, and the belief in one's own enchantment breaks out everywhere. . . . And here is the cradle of drama. For the latter begins . . . inasmuch as man is outside himself [ausser sich] and believes himself to be transformed and enchanted. In the state of "being outside himself," of ecstasy [des "Ausser sich seins," der Ecstase] only one further step is necessary: [that] we turn back again into ourselves but rather enter into another being so that we behave as if enchanted . . . : the ground becomes unsteady, the belief in the indissolvability and rigidity of the individual. (III 2: 11–12)

Let the Dionysian state, the Dionysian impulse, be taken, then, as one of *ecstasy*, of being outside oneself. Dionysian ecstasy would arise in excess, producing such enchantment that one would no longer turn back into oneself but, entering into the other, would disrupt the very delimitation of the individual.[10] The Dionysian

10. There are additional notebook entries that draw much the same connection. For instance, in a note written between the end of 1870 and April 1871 one finds an earlier draft of a discussion that was to appear in section 10 of *The Birth of Tragedy*, namely, the discussion of the dual nature of Dionysus, of his

would be both a state (*Zustand*) and an impulse (*Trieb*), both at once, the state of the individual reveler who is so impelled outside himself as to violate the very limits of individuality.

Let me focus on this figure of ecstasy precisely as *at once* outlining both state and impulse. It is a figure that releases a strange logic, and it is in this logic that one can discern the capacity of the Dionysian to resist stabilization along the metaphysical axis.

In Dionysian ecstasy, in being outside oneself, one transgresses the limit that ordinarily would delimit one's self, one's individuality, one's subjectivity. The Dionysian state is one of being impelled beyond the limit, driven on beyond the very limit that would delimit every state of the individual. Such transgression of the limit cannot but disrupt the limit and the delimitation that it effects. In being outside oneself, one's being a self—the oneself that would be delimited by that inside in opposition to which one would be outside oneself—would not simply remain intact and determinate; it would cease to remain so precisely insofar as one would *be outside* oneself. Nietzsche himself marks this disruption: as Dionysian emotions "grow in intensity, the subjective vanishes into complete self-oblivion [*Selbstvergessenheit*]" (III 1: 25).[11] Di-

---

dismemberment by the Titans and of his rebirth as the end of individuation. What one finds only in the earlier draft, in the midst of this discussion, is the phrase: "those ecstatic states [*jene ekstatischen Zustände*]" (III 3: 186). Another note from the same period refers to the Dionysian as welling up from the power of nature without the mediation of the artist; such "Dionysian excitement" is then said to be "born in those ecstatic festivals of Spring [*in jenen ekstatischen Frühlingfesten geboren*]" (III 3: 198). Another note from fall 1869 characterizes "the root of drama" as "the excited ecstatic carnival mood [*die aufgeregte extatische Faschingslaune*]" (III 3: 7). See also III 3: 52–53. The 1870 lectures on *Oedipus Tyrannos* also explicitly connect the Dionysian with ecstasy, introducing the Dionysian as "ecstatic excitement" and "forgetting of individuality." Nietzsche continues: "The ecstatic state in the Dionysian spring festivals is the birthplace of music and of the dithyramb. . . . With those initiated into the service of Bacchus . . . the soul was displaced outside itself [*ausser sich versetzt*]. In this state it entered into another being, and belief in enchantment was universal" (W 17: 297).

11. In "The Dionysian Worldview" Nietzsche refers to two forces, the impulse of spring and the narcotic draught, that drive the naive natural man to the self-oblivion of frenzy (*zur Selbstvergessenheit des Rausches*). He continues: "Their effects are symbolized in the figure of Dionysus. In both conditions the *principium individuationis* is breached; the subjective disappears completely in the face of the erupting force of the universally human, indeed of the universally

onysian ecstasy would not be a matter simply of relating an inside
to an outside; it would not be a relation that would supervene upon
an opposition that would remain essentially unaffected by it.
Rather, insofar as in ecstasy one would come to *be outside* oneself,
the oneself that it would be the function of the inside to delimit
would be displaced from inside to outside; and this displacement
could not but disrupt the very operation of the opposition, for the
inside is nothing but the inside *of* the self. Thus, in ecstasy transgression cannot but disrupt the limit. And yet, transgression is
possible only in relation to the limit; that is, one can be *outside
oneself* only if the self within continues somehow to be delimited.
And so, to disrupt the limit definitive of the opposition would be
to disrupt the very limit by which the transgression, the being outside, would be defined.

Let it be said, then, that Dionysian ecstasy is an *exceeding* of the
limit that would delimit the self, an exceeding in the dual sense of
transgression and disruption. Thus is expressed in the logic of the
Dionysian the dual nature of the god: reunion and dismemberment
as transgression and disruption. The logic of being outside oneself,
the logical dynamics of the figure of ecstasy, is such that, as transgression, it cannot but disrupt the very limit by which it would be
defined; hence, in turn, there can be transgressive disruption of the
limit only if the limit is also redrawn, reinstated, as the very limit
to be transgressed. The logic of the figure is such as to generate an
unending round of transgression, disruption, and reinstatement.

Such is, then, ecstatic logic: a logic of reiterated duality, of the
duality of transgression and disruption and of disruption and reinstatement. It is a logic to be written only by way of a certain
duality, which has already been in play without my having, up to
this point, marked it, a duality of effacement and (re)inscription, a
crossing of what is said with an unsaying—in short, a double
writing.

The character of the Dionysian as ecstasy is what determines its
peculiar opposition to the Apollinian. In the latter there is an installing of measure, of a measure by which to draw around oneself, as it were, the limit of an individuality. The drawing of this
limit and the drawing of oneself into it constitute Apollinian self-

---

natural" (III 2: 46–47). See the corresponding formulation in *The Birth of
Tragedy* (III 1: 24–25).

knowledge. To this Apollinian measure the votaries of Dionysus oppose *excess* (*Übermass*). For in its character as ecstasy the Dionysian state/impulse is excess itself, excess as such, the very moment of exceeding; or, more precisely, the Dionysian is what one would call excess *itself*, excess *as such*, were not the excess such as to disrupt the very operation of such delimitation as would be presupposed by the *as such*, by the *itself*—hence, again, the need for a crossing of saying with unsaying. In reference to the self, the Dionysian is the exceeding of the limit by which one's individuality would be delimited, by which the self would be defined and constituted as an interior space of self-possession. Such exceeding is thus a disruption of determinate selfhood, a certain loss of self—let it be called: an abysmal loss of self. It is thus that Nietzsche repeatedly relates the Dionysian to terror, dread, suffering (*Schrecken, Entsetzlichkeit, Leiden*). It is not that the Dionysian produces or discloses terror, dread, suffering; rather, the Dionysian *is* to the utmost extent that loss of self, of self-possession and measure, that one undergoes in various degrees and connections when one is struck with terror, possessed by dread, or overcome with suffering. And yet, the logic of the Dionysian, the logic of the dual, is such as to intertwine such loss with the joy, the jubilation, the pleasure of transgressive reunion.

The opposition between Apollinian and Dionysian is not, then, a simple binary opposition. Already it has been noted how the opening paragraph of *The Birth of Tragedy* describes this opposition as one "which the common term 'art' only seemingly bridges." It is by no means an opposition merely of species to be united under the generic term *art* (or, in the case of the natural impulses, *proto-art*); rather, it is an opposition that threatens, that in a sense suspends, the very unity of the word *art*, hence, too, the unity of that aesthetic science that Nietzsche proposes to advance. "The Dionysian Worldview" extends the threat, the suspension, to the word *poetry* (*Poesie*), which, since it encompasses both the Apollinian epic and the Dionysian lyric, is denied the status of a category coordinate with formative art (*die bildende Kunst*) and music and is designated instead as a conglutinate of two very different art impulses (III 2: 56). The opposition between Apollinian and Dionysian, threatening the coherence of the very language of aesthetics, is a monstrous opposition (*ein ungeheurer Gegensatz*).

Thus, the Apollinian and the Dionysian are not binary opposites; neither is their relation, transposed to the order of language, one of contradiction. At least not unless it is a matter of such contradiction as that of which Nietzsche writes as follows: "Contradiction, the bliss born of pain, spoke out from the heart of nature" (III 1: 37). For such contradiction as this is both more and less than contradiction: it is a contradiction in which the opposites are held in their opposition rather than cancelling one another, and it is a contradiction that is not simply unsaid in being said but that is spoken out from the heart of nature. [12]

The relation between the Apollinian and the Dionysian is not, then, merely the opposition between production of limit and disruption of limit. Rather, the Dionysian is the dual movement of transgressing the limit of self and of disrupting (in that very transgression) the very limit by which the transgression would be determined, the limit whose reinstatement would thus always have to recommence. Granted the complexity of these intertwinings, one might say that the Dionysian is a certain movement at the limit. The complexity of this movement, hence of the relation of the Dionysian to the Apollinian, is what, most of all, prohibits regarding tragedy as the mere synthesis of the Apollinian and the Dionysian, as a synthesis in which their opposition would be resolved into a higher unity—in a word: *aufgehoben*. The logic of Apollinian and Dionysian, the logic that governs the inscription and effacement of Nietzsche's text, is not a logic of *Aufhebung*, not a dialectic, but a logic of excess, of resounding excess, of shining excess. [13]

12. The preliminary essays and notes of the period do not always completely avoid suggesting that the Apollinian and the Dionysian are simple opposites. For example, one note characterizes the Dionysian as "the complete opposite [*den vollen Gegensatz*]" of the Apollinian, opposing them as "*Schein des Seins*" to "*Schein des Scheins*" (III 3: 192). "The Dionysian Worldview" refers to the myth according to which "Apollo put the dismembered Dionysus back together again" (III 2: 51). Yet, what may here be taken as simple opposition is, nonetheless, presented as the relation of Apollo only to one side of the god, not to Dionysus in his dual nature.

13. Thus it does not suffice to submit the reading of *The Birth of Tragedy* solely to the grid provided by Nietzsche's remark in *Ecce Homo* that the work smells offensively Hegelian, that it has the smell of antitheses (Apollinian/Dionysian) being *aufgehoben* into a unity (VI 3: 308). Consequently, *The Birth of Tragedy* is not to be differentiated from Nietzsche's later writings in the manner proposed, for example, by Gilles Deleuze (*La Philosophie de Nietzsche* [Paris: Presses Universitaires de France, 1962], chap. 1), namely, by its alleged dialectical, hence thoroughly metaphysical character.

Here is how Nietzsche sketches the opposition, describing the intrusion of the Dionysian into the world of the Apollinian Greeks:

And now let us consider how into this world built on shining [*Schein*] and moderation [*Mässigung*] and artificially damned up, there rang out in ever more alluring and magical ways the ecstatic sound [*der ekstatische Ton*] of the Dionysian festival; how in these all of nature's excess [*Übermass*] in pleasure, suffering, and knowledge became audible, even in piercing shrieks; . . . The muses of the arts of "shining" [*"Schein"*] paled before an art that, in its frenzy [*Rausch*], spoke the truth. The wisdom of Silenus cried "Woe! woe!" to the serene Olympians. The individual, with all his limits and restraint [*mit allen seinen Grenzen und Massen*] succumbed to the self-oblivion [*Selbstvergessenheit*] of the Dionysian states, forgetting the Apollinian precepts. *Excess* revealed itself as truth [Das Übermass *enthüllte sich als Wahrheit*]. (III 1: 36–37)[14]

Dionysian revelation overwhelms the Apollinian, sweeping away its limits and its moderation: excess revealed itself as truth. It revealed itself not just as *a* truth, as something true, for Dionysian ecstasy in its very exceeding of limits dissolves the determinateness by which something would be determined as true; or, rather, it sets those limits and determinations within an uncontrollable circuit of disruption and reinstatement. Dionysian excess revealed itself not even as a *fundamental* truth, not even as *the* fundamental truth, the truth by which all others would be grounded. For one could take Dionysian excess to be such a ground, to underlie all truths or things as their ground, as the origin from which they would arise in their determination, only at the cost of ignoring the way in which the would-be ground disrupts the very ordering that belongs to the concept of ground and dissolves the very determinateness that ground would produce.

Let it be said, then, that what Dionysian revelation reveals is not a ground of determination but the dissolution of ground and of determination. What is revealed is not ground but *abyss*. The revelation leaves one "gazing into the Dionysian abysses" (III 1: 88).

14. In "The Dionysian Worldview" there is a slightly different version of this passage. Two differences in the unpublished text should be noted. (1) It reads: "an art that, in its ecstatic frenzy [*in ihrem ekstatischen Rausche*] spoke the truth." (2) It contains, following the sentence about the individual's succumbing to the self-oblivion of the Dionysian states, the following: "a twilight of the gods [*eine Götterdämmerung*] was close at hand" (III 2: 57–58).

One could say, doubling the saying with an unsaying: excess is the truth that is, at once, the dissolution of truth. Let it be called: abysmal truth. Let it also be recalled from the saying, recalled into the circuit of effacement and reinscription.[15]

It will be necessary later to consider that other truth that among the Greeks came to oppose the excess of the Dionysian, bringing tragedy thus to its end. But even without yet undertaking to thematize Socratism in its opposition to tragedy, it will be helpful to cast a glance ahead to that turn inscribed in the Platonic dialogues by which was opened the space of metaphysics.

Here, too, it is a matter of a turn away from the everyday: not, however, toward the abyss but rather toward ground and determination. It is of this turn that Socrates tells in the *Phaedo,* where he speaks in the face of death, under the threat of the abyss of abysses. It is the turn by which he came to his characteristic way of questioning, the turn through which, in word and in deed, he sought to lead the young philosopher (Glaucon) in the *Republic.* It is a turn away from the everyday, from what presents itself immediately and to some extent always indeterminately; a turn to the εἶδος as the pure determinacy that shines through things, empowering their showing and hence constituting their ground and their truth. The Socratic turn thus opens the space between what come to be called the sensible and the intelligible, beings and their Being. It is within this space that metaphysics will move, at least according to the story that Nietzsche will tell more and more clearly and finally in the form of the narrative, "How the 'True World' Finally Became a Fable." Any thinking that would turn outside this space, that would exceed the sphere of Being and beings, would be oriented toward the beyond of Being (ἐπέκεινα τῆς οὐσίας), not aligned with the axis of metaphysics. In undertaking to think the Dionysian as ecstasy and abyss, Nietzsche broaches such excessive thinking, a thinking that exposes itself to *das Masslose.*

15. Eugen Fink gestures in the direction of such an abysmal reading, regarding the Dionysian revelation as an "openness to the dark nightside of life" (Eugen Fink, *Nietzsches Philosophie* [Stuttgart: Kohlhammer, 1960], 28). Nonetheless, he stops short of detaching the Dionysian from the concept of ground, referring thus to the Dionysian ground, characterizing it even as a *"Hinterwelt"* (ibid., 27).

C

And yet, is *The Birth of Tragedy* so excessive? Does Nietzsche's thinking of the Dionysian turn outside, turn against, exceed, the space of the Platonic difference between intelligible and sensible? Or does it not remain situated precisely within the compass of that distinction in the guise that it assumes beginning with Kant, as the distinction between thing-in-itself and appearance? Or even in its Schopenhauerian guise, as the distinction between the will (as the thing-in-itself) and appearances produced through the operation of representation? Is the fundamental distinction of *The World as Will and Representation*, the distinction that reinscribes the metaphysical order of fundament, that is, of ground—is this distinction not reinscribed in *The Birth of Tragedy?* And does this reinscription not serve finally to limit the excess of Nietzsche's thinking, to turn that thinking back away from *das Masslose*, back to the security of metaphysics?

Is it not indicative that even Heidegger—whose reading of Nietzsche first produced the very terms of these questions and redetermined irrevocably the very space of all subsequent reading—tends to regard *The Birth of Tragedy* as having been largely determined by Schopenhauer's theory of the will?[16] Is it not also indicative that Eugen Fink—in dialogue with Heidegger's reading and oriented toward a certain recovery of Nietzsche's thinking from the space of metaphysics—regards the Schopenhauerian distinction between will and representation as still operative in *The Birth of Tragedy*, even if no longer as a demarcation between two separate regions but rather as structuring the originary ποίησις of cosmic life?[17]

16. "At first Schopenhauer's theory of the will governs Nietzsche's thinking" (Martin Heidegger, *Vorträge und Aufsätze* [Pfullingen: Verlag Günther Neske, 1954], 83). On the other hand, Heidegger's reading is often more nuanced, more sensitive to the dislocation to which traditional concepts are frequently subjected in Nietzsche's texts. For example, in the lecture course "The Will to Power as Art" he cites a later note in which Nietzsche refers to the proclamation, set forth in *The Birth of Tragedy*, that art is the properly metaphysical activity of this life. Heidegger comments: "'Life' is not only meant in the narrow sense of human life but is identified with 'world' in the Schopenhauerian sense. The statement is reminiscent of Schopenhauer, but it is already speaking against him" (*Nietzsche*, 1: 86).

17. "The ontological distinction that Nietzsche takes over from Schopenhauer as 'will' and 'representation' (or 'thing-in-itself' and 'appearance') is not taken as a

I have called attention already to the operation of the Schopenhauerian distinction in Nietzsche's discussion of the Apollinian,
noting, at the same time, certain gaps, certain cross-purposes, as
well as Nietzsche's own reference to the Schopenhauerian framework as a "metaphysical assumption" and his acknowledgment
that he is applying the words of Schopenhauer to the Apollinian
"in an eccentric sense." Yet even granting these limitations as regards the operation of Schopenhauer's metaphysics in the
determination of the Apollinian, one still cannot but ask whether
that metaphysics is not massively and decisively operative in
Nietzsche's thinking of the Dionysian. For example, when
Nietzsche writes of the Dionysian: "Now, with the gospel of world
harmony, each one feels himself not only united, reconciled, and
fused with his neighbor, but as one with him, as if the veil of maya
had been torn asunder and were now merely fluttering in tatters
before the mysterious primal one" (III 1: 25–26). Does not the an-
nihilating reunion of the individual, his fusion with others and
with nature, enact a return of appearances toward the noumenal
ground? Would not the Dionysian state be one of virtual unification with the primal one, with the will itself? Would not the
Dionysian be a movement toward the metaphysical center, toward
the ground, and not, finally, at the limit, not at all toward the
abyss?

The supposition that *The Birth of Tragedy* is determined by
Schopenhauer's metaphysics seems only to be strengthened if one
turns to Nietzsche's correspondence between the time of his discov-
ery of Schopenhauer's work in 1865[18] and that of the publication of
The Birth of Tragedy in 1872. Thus, writing to Gersdorff in August
1866, he refers to Schopenhauer, "for whom I still have every sym-

---

demarcation between two separate regions; rather it is interpreted as a *movement,* as
a creative process. The primal ground plays the world [*Der Urgrund spielt Welt*]; it
brings forth the multiplicity of particular beings—as the artist brings forth the
work. Or better: the activity of the artist, his creative process, is only a mirror
image and a faint repetition of the most originary ποίησις of cosmic life" (Fink,
Nietzsches Philosophie, 30).

18. Shortly thereafter Nietzsche wrote an autobiographical sketch in which
he describes how he discovered Schopenhauer's work while browsing one day in
a Leipzig bookshop: in this book, he says, "I saw a mirror in which I beheld the
world, life, and my mind depicted in frightful grandeur" (*Werke in drei Bänden,*
ed. K. Schlechta [München: Carl Hanser Verlag, 1954–56], 3: 133).

pathy"; and though Nietzsche touches upon certain difficulties with the concept of the thing-in-itself (as "the final product of an antithesis that is determined by our organization"), he appears to regard them as somehow only serving to enhance the appeal of Schopenhauer. He concludes: "I know of no more edifying philosopher than our Schopenhauer" (BKG I 2: 159–60). Writing again to Gersdorff in April 1869, he refers to "that Schopenhauerian seriousness" and declares: "my philosophical seriousness is already too deeply rooted, too clearly have the true and essential problems of life and thought been shown to me by the great mystagogue Schopenhauer" (BKG I 2: 386). To Gersdorff again in September of the same year: the Schopenhauerian "worldview permeates my thinking more and more every day" (BKG II 1: 60). Once again to Gersdorff in March 1870: "For me, all that is best and most beautiful is associated with the names Schopenhauer and Wagner" (BKG II 1: 105).

In 1874, two years after the publication of *The Birth of Tragedy,* Nietzsche devoted one of his four *Untimely Meditations* to Schopenhauer. In *Schopenhauer as Educator* he writes of his master: "I trusted him at once and my trust is the same now as it was nine years ago" (III 1: 342)—that is, in the year when he first discovered Schopenhauer's work. In this testimony—and indeed throughout this text—one cannot but notice that Nietzsche's praise is for Schopenhauer the teacher, not for the philosophical doctrines that he teaches but rather for the existential stance that his example conveys. For Nietzsche, Schopenhauer is an educator who could teach him "again to be *simple* and *honest* in thought and life, thus to be untimely, that word understood in the profoundest sense" (III 1: 342). Nietzsche praises Schopenhauer for "his honesty, his cheerfulness, and his steadfastness" (III 1: 346) while remaining virtually silent about the content of Schopenhauer's philosophy. The situation is aptly described in a recent paper by Michel Haar: "The 'trust' is addressed solely to the man, exemplary for his 'heroism of truth' . . . . In effect, this *Third Untimely Meditation* which ought, in principle, to render homage to a great thinker, remains strangely discreet about the *ideas* of this hero of thought: scarcely any allusions to his doctrine!"[19]

19. Haar goes on to point to three reasons why Nietzsche's admiration for Schopenhauer persisted: (1) Nietzsche continued to regard Schopenhauer as the

When, on the other hand, Nietzsche addresses the doctrines of Schopenhauer's metaphysics, the entire tone is different. For example, in a note written in 1878, in utter contrast to the profession of trust cited above: "My distrust against his system was there from the beginning" (IV 3: 382). Another note, written in the mid-1880s (apparently as part of a draft for a preface for the new edition of *The Birth of Tragedy*) and published in *The Will to Power*, addresses with utter directness the question of the involvement of the metaphysical distinction in *The Birth of Tragedy:* "The antithesis of a real and an apparent world is lacking here: there is only *one* world, and this is false, cruel, contradictory, seductive, without meaning" (WM §853). Little wonder that the "Attempt at a Self-Critique" (which actually became the preface to the new edition of *The Birth of Tragedy*) withdraws the Schopenhauerian formulas from the "strange and new valuations that were basically at odds with . . . Schopenhauer's spirit and taste" (III 1: 13). By the time of *Ecce Homo* Nietzsche will declare: "the cadaverous perfume of Schopenhauer sticks only to a few formulas" (VI 3: 308).

And yet, it is not only retrospectively that Nietzsche would set Schopenhauer's metaphysics at a distance from the thought of *The Birth of Tragedy*. Indeed, his distrust was there from the beginning, expressed in a series of remarkable notes written between September 1870 and April 1871—that is, at the very threshold of *The Birth of Tragedy*. Still more remarkably, his critical distance from Schopenhauer is also fully expressed in an even earlier text entitled "Fragment of a Critique of the Schopenhauerian Philosophy" (M 1: 392–401). The probable date of this text is 1867. Even a brief reading of it will suffice to show that Nietzsche had already decisively distanced himself from Schopenhauer's metaphysics within a couple of years of discovering it and some five years before the publication of *The Birth of Tragedy*.

The text begins with a reference to the title of Schopenhauer's

---

one who decisively revealed to him his vocation; (2) Schopenhauer was the one who brought Nietzsche to discover the power of *nonhistorical* life; (3) Schopenhauer was the first philosopher to be an avowed and inflexible atheist, and this for Nietzsche was demonstrative of his honesty. On the other hand, Haar distinguishes clearly between Nietzsche's admiration for Schopenhauer at this level and his critical attitude toward Schopenhauer's metaphysics ("La rupture initiale de Nietzsche avec Schopenhauer," in *Schopenhauer et la force du pessimisme* [Monaco: Éditions de Rocher, 1988], esp. 103–4).

work: *The World as Will and Representation*. The young Nietzsche observes that this title expresses Schopenhauer's fundamental view: "When brought under the apparatus of representation, the groundless, knowledgeless will reveals itself as world" (M 1: 392). Nietzsche notes Schopenhauer's expressed solidarity with Kant, specifically with the Kantian distinction between appearance and thing-in-itself. He remarks that when one subtracts from Schopenhauer what he has taken over from Kant, "there remains the one word 'will,' together with its predicates" (M 1: 392).

Declaring the errors of great men to be more worthy of honor than the truths of little men, Nietzsche turns to his critique. Schopenhauer can, he says, be attacked from four sides.

First, Nietzsche charges that, as with Kant, the concept of the thing-in-itself is "merely a concealed category" (M 1: 394). This is to say that the thing-in-itself is not something existing behind appearances and independently of thought but that, no less than causality, for example, it is posited by thought. In this criticism Nietzsche's overall strategy against Schopenhauer begins to take shape: to declare the thing-in-itself a concealed category is to threaten the very distinction between thing-in-itself and appearance, to broach a collapse of the thing-in-itself into appearances.

The second criticism continues the assault on the thing-in-itself by calling into question Schopenhauer's identification of it as the will: what Schopenhauer "puts in place of the Kantian x, namely, the will, is engendered only with the help of a poetic intuition" (M 1: 394). The criticism can easily be underwritten by reference to Schopenhauer's text, most notably, to the beginning of the Second Book, where Schopenhauer presents a kind of argument for his identification of the thing-in-itself as will. It is for essential reasons an argument that Schopenhauer presents in first person, since it is centered in the peculiar identity of the I. The argument begins, specifically, with the identity of the body and the will: every act of will is at once a movement of the body—that is, an act cannot be willed without one's being aware that it appears as a movement of one's body. Thus, one's will and one's body (Schopenhauer often writes, more precisely: my will and my body) are not two different states connected by causality "but are one and the same thing, though given in two entirely different ways" (WWV 1: §18). Schopenhauer assimilates the identity to the Kantian dichotomy: the body in itself, as thing-in-itself, is simply will. Then, in the most decisive move of the argument, Schopenhauer proposes to use this double knowledge that one has of oneself (as body and as will, the two recognized in their identity); he proposes to use it *as* "the key to the inner being [*Wesen*] of every appearance in nature" (WWV 1: §19); that is, he proposes to take the inner nature of all other things (what they are as things-in-themselves) to be also will. What is most remarkable is that—despite the semblance of argumentation—he gives no reason for this move (or, rather, this leap) except to say that besides will and representation there is nothing else conceivable for us; but even if this were so, it would hardly justify the move. Thus Nietzsche's critique, which says in effect that it is not a cognitive or theoretical move at all but a poetic intuition: "the attempted logical proof can satisfy neither Schopenhauer nor us" (M 1: 394).

The third critique concerns the attributes ascribed by Schopenhauer to the will: "We must protest against the predicates that Schopenhauer attributes to his will, which, for something utterly unthinkable, sound much too determinate and are derived from the opposition to the world of representation; whereas between the thing-in-itself and the appearance the concept of opposition does not have any meaning" (M 1: 394). Nietzsche's critique is easily underwritten by considering some of the predicates that Schopenhauer attributes to the will: the will is one in the sense of being "free from all plurality," of lying "outside the possibility of plurality" (WWV 1: §23); it is indivisible (§25); it is not dispersed in space (§25), indeed "lies outside time and space" (§23); it is unmoved in the midst of change (§28); and an "absence of all aim, of all limits [*Grenzen*], belongs to the inner nature [*Wesen*] of the will-in-itself" (§29). In all of these instances the simple oppositional thinking that is operative is all too obtrusive: the attributes ascribed to the will are simply the binary opposites of the attributes of appearances. Yet none of these examples makes the matter so abundantly clear as does the following bizarre instance:

But we also find that the *inner necessity* of the gradation of the will's phenomena, inseparable from the adequate objectivity of the will, is expressed by an *outer necessity* in the whole of these phenomena themselves. By virtue of such necessity, man needs the animals for his support, the animals in their grades need one another, and also the plants, which again need soil, water, chemical elements and their combinations, the planet, the sun, rotation and motion around the sun, the obliquity of the ecliptic, and so on. At bottom, this springs from the fact that the will must live on itself, since nothing exists besides it, and it is a hungry will. Hence arise pursuit, hunting, anxiety, and suffering. (WWV 1: §28)

Finally, Nietzsche extends the third critique: "All the predicates of the will are taken from the world of appearance" (M 1: 397). He could have referred, most effectively, to the self-cannibalism attributed to the will in the passage just cited. But, instead, he refers to unity, eternity, and freedom, expressing his doubt whether these can have any meaning outside the sphere of human knowledge, that is, outside the world of appearances. One might say, then, that in Schopenhauer's discourse on the thing-in-itself as will, that thing comes to be thoroughly contaminated by the very appearances to which it is opposed; simple opposition to appearances cannot but draw its content precisely from that to which it is opposed.

The result is that the very distinction between thing-in-itself and appearance is threatened. In fact, Nietzsche's critique concludes by analyzing Schopenhauer's theory of the intellect in such a way as to attempt to show that the distinction between the will and the world as represented by the intellect (that is, the world of appearances) cannot be sustained. Borrowing the title from *Twilight of the Idols* (1888), one may say that already in this very early text, already well in advance of *The Birth of Tragedy*, it is announced that the "true world" has finally become a fable.

Yet, even without referring to the early text, one could trace much the same critique in various passages from Nietzsche's notebooks of the period September 1870–April 1871. Here, too, Nietzsche's critique is aimed at Schopenhauer's fundamental distinction. This aim is clear in the following extract from one of the longer notes:

In the will there is plurality and movement only by means of representation: an eternal being becomes becoming, becomes will, only through representation. . . . Representation is thus the birth of the will; plurality is thus already in the will. (III 3: 117–18)

Another note draws explicitly the consequence of installing representation and plurality within the will:

If a representation must be bound up with the will, then the will is also not an expression for the core of nature. (III 3: 119)

The will is, then, no thing-in-itself over against representation and appearance. Its purity, its remoteness, cannot be sustained.

Another note testifies to the contamination that will always already have drawn the will into the sphere of appearances:

We recognize that core only as representations; we are acquainted with it only in its expression in images: moreover, there is never a direct bridge that would lead us to it itself. Even our entire instinctive life [*Triebleben*], the play of feelings, sensations, affects, acts of will, is, on closer examination, known to us—as I must insert here against Schopenhauer—only as representation, not in its inner being [*Wesen*]: and we ought indeed to say that even the "will" of Schopenhauer is nothing but the most general form of appearance of something otherwise totally inscrutable to us. (III 3: 378–79)

Even the Schopenhauerian "will" is nothing but appearance, requiring thus the quotation marks that serve to cross out the very opposition on which its sense depends but which in this discourse is being disrupted; and which, again—not without a certain irony—is being reconstituted by the reference beyond to a thing-in-itself that would really be such and that could have nothing whatsoever to do with the will. In the experience of the will, one has no access to a thing-in-itself, no double knowledge of oneself that could, even if by a leap, be taken as the key to the knowledge of all things. Another note is still more direct:

There is no path for man to the primal one. He is completely appearance. (III 3: 213)

Or again:

The will already a form of appearance. (III 3: 211)

In the wake of Nietzsche's massive critique of Schopenhauer prior to 1872, which poses again and again the collapse of the fundamental distinction of Schopenhauer's metaphysics, there can be no question of a reading that would begin by assimilating *The Birth of Tragedy* to that metaphysical axis; thus I have proposed a reading that commences instead, as regards the Dionysian, with an orientation to a figure of ecstasy that cannot be aligned with that axis. And yet, the difficulty is that Nietzsche himself, despite the critique, invokes the metaphysical axis at several major junctures in *The Birth of Tragedy*. If indeed there is no path for man to the primal one, if indeed he is completely appearance, then how is it that Nietzsche can declare in *The Birth of Tragedy* that the "Dionysian artist has become completely one with the primal one" (III 1: 39–40)? If, still more radically, the primal one, the thing-in-itself, is merely a concealed category posited by naive oppositional thinking, how is it that, nonetheless, Nietzsche can invoke the very distinction between thing-in-itself and appearance and proclaim that tragedy "points to the eternal life of this core of existence that abides through the perpetual destruction of appearances" (III 1: 55)?

How, then, is one to read the reinscription of Schopenhauer's metaphysics in *The Birth of Tragedy?* Is it only a result of Nietzsche's wish to spare the sensibilities of Wagner and of others of his friends who were ardent partisans of Schopenhauer?[20] Or is the reentry of the metaphysical axis into *The Birth of Tragedy* only a matter of a formula, a borrowed vocabulary, from which the work remains essentially free and from which in the later "Attempt at a Self-Critique" it can be in fact detached?[21] Or is there also some essential reason for the reinscription?

It is too early to tell, at least as long as the positive role explicitly ascribed to Schopenhauer's philosophy by *The Birth of Tragedy* has not been discussed. Whatever the case may be, there can be no question of massive assimilation. Nietzsche's text cannot but have twisted free from the Schopenhauerian metaphysical axis. It is only a question of whether there is a structural necessity that links the reinscription to that twisting.

d

A certain twisting commences as soon as the question of Dionysian art comes into play. The classical schema of mimesis that Nietzsche

20. Haar raises this possibility and concludes indecisively: "It is a probable, but psychological interpretation" (ibid., 111).

21. This interpretation is argued forcefully (and without reference to earlier notes and fragments) by David Allison: "What was at issue, then, in the later preface was to show that his earlier analysis was only *nominally* defective; despite the borrowed vocabulary, Nietzsche argued that his account in *The Birth of Tragedy* remained consistent and valid, that it in no way committed him to the metaphysical tenets of Schopenhauer and Kant. . . . 'The Dionysian' was indeed all-too-humanly empirical. It was the affective register of ecstasy, of intense delight and suffering, everywhere experienced throughout the ancient world" ("Nietzsche Knows No Noumenon," in *Why Nietzsche Now?* ed. Daniel O'Hara, [Bloomington: Indiana University Press, 1985], 304).

laid out initially would prescribe that Dionysian art arise as mimesis of that Dionysian energy that will always have burst forth from nature prior to the advent of the human artist. Dionysian art would consist in mimesis of the natural Dionysian state. And yet, the Dionysian is both state and impulse, both at once in their very opposition, the state of one impelled outside himself in violation of the very limit that would define the state and the self—in a word, ecstasy. In Dionysian art the artist would produce a mimetic double of Dionysian ecstasy—that is, Dionysian art would be mimesis of ecstasy. And yet, the conjunction of mimesis and ecstasy cannot but submit the classical schema of mimesis to a certain deformation, redetermining both the productive relation of the artist and the mimetic relation of the artwork; it cannot but also produce a certain dislocating effect in the language of Nietzsche's text, beginning to twist that text free of the metaphysical axis by making its language slide in another direction, toward the abyss.

But is it indeed ecstasy that is doubled in Dionysian mimesis? Must one not address the philosophical question to the Dionysian, asking what it is, inquiring—even if with a certain suspension— about its abysmal identity? Especially in view of what Nietzsche writes, in reference to the lyrist:

First of all, as a Dionysian artist he has become completely one with the primal one, its pain and contradiction, and he produces the copy of this primal one as music, assuming that music has been correctly termed a repetition and a recast of the world. (III 1: 39–40)

Is it not, then, indisputable that the Dionysian original is the primal one? Or, at least, that it is to be called the *primal one?* Is this not indisputably the name of the origin, even if it is into ecstasy that the Dionysian reveler and indeed the Dionysian artist are thrown? Even if in one of the notebooks Nietzsche says directly (almost as if ignoring Apollinian art): "All art requires a 'being outside oneself,' an ἔκστασις" (III 3: 52)? Is the distance between these two, between the one and ecstasy, irreducible? Is *the one* simply the name of the origin to which, in being outside oneself, one would return? Or does the one also undergo the dislocating effect that the very inscription of ecstasy produces?

Even in Schopenhauer's text the language and concept of the primal one undergo a certain slippage, even if the effects of that slippage are massively repressed. On the one hand, the Schopenhauerian thing-in-itself, the will, is declared to be one, to be outside the very possibility of plurality (WWV 1: §23). And yet, it is also said to involve variance with itself (*Entzweiung mit sich selbst*) (§27); indeed this variance would be the noumenal ground of that universal struggle and conflict to which so much of *The World as Will and Representation* is addressed and from which art is said to provide a certain deliverance. Need one say what the word itself already says: *Entzweiung,* variance with itself, violates the allegedly unconditional oneness of the will. Not only can a will at variance with itself not be outside the possibility of plurality, but also it must harbor within itself both the possibility and the actuality of plurality.

Nietzsche extends this self-variance, extends it in the language of contradiction. Thus Nietzsche writes of the Dionysian artist that "he has become completely one with the primal one, *its pain and contradiction*" (III 1: 39–40—emphasis added). Within the primal one there would be that contradiction that is both more and less than contradiction, the contradiction of bliss born of pain, the contradiction in which joy and suffering, reunion and dismemberment, are held together in their very opposition. Because it is thus sundered, thus dual-natured, Nietzsche can declare in the notebooks: "Insofar as contradiction is the essence of the primal one, it also can be at the same time both the highest suffering and the highest joy" (III 3: 207).

Yet, even if it cannot but broach plurality, even if it must be of such extent as to include contradiction, retaining opposites in their very opposition, nonetheless, it is called *one* both by Schopenhauer and by Nietzsche. And yet, Schopenhauer says that it is not one as an object—an individual—is one. For the oneness of an object is known only by opposition to a possible plurality: it is a oneness in which a plurality of determinations is unified. The one, on the other hand, is, he says, outside the possibility of plurality. Is it, then, to be identified as a pure one in the sense of a single determination, a concept? Schopenhauer refuses also this identification: it "is one not as a concept is one, for a concept originates only through abstraction from a plurality" (WWV 1: §23). A determination is inseparable from those others to which it is opposed, that is, determination is negation. But then, the one neither is determined (as an individual in which a plurality of determinations is unified and localized); nor is it even just a determination, *a* determinate one independent of the *principium individuationis.* It is not even just the determination: one. Rather, it is one only as utter dissolution of determination. It is nothing delimitable—that is, nothing but one, a one that is nothing. It is nothing but the opposite of the plurality of determinate appearances—a pure opposite, that is, a vacuous opposite. In this form it could offer not the slightest resistance to the massive critique that Nietzsche has prepared in those early fragments discussed above. If—without simply suppressing the fact of the reinscription—that critique is now brought into play, then what is called—improperly—*the primal one (das Ureine)* must be drawn back into the domain of appearances, redrawn there as the figure of dissolution of the limits determining individuals. But then it would be nothing other than the figure of ecstasy, the abysmal movement of indeterminacy, the circuit of transgression, disruption, and reinstatement. It is the movement of excess, of Dionysian truth.

Thus, the identity of the Dionysian would not lie in some originary being over against the individual, who in Dionysian ecstasy would then return to this origin. For there is no origin, and the Dionysian has only an abysmal identity: the movement, the figure, of ecstasy. At least such must be its identity as long as the massive critique of Schopenhauer's metaphysics is kept in play. But this will also require deferring still the question of the reinscription, thus undercutting and displacing the metaphysical language that tends to obtrude most of all when Nietzsche's text turns toward the Dionysian: as when the Dionysian artist is said to become one with the primal one.

What is thus said is, then, to say: the Dionysian artist undergoes a certain self-oblivion, a loss of self, as he is cast into ecstasy with its transgression and disruption of the limits definitive of the self. The Dionysian artist is one who has "surrendered his subjectivity in the Dionysian process" (III 1: 40); this is why Dionysian art cannot be regarded as subjective and thus contrasted with Apollinian art in terms of the opposition between subjective and objective. If it can be said that lyric poetry, commencing as Dionysian art, begins with a certain death of the author, such death is to be thought ecstatically and not metaphysically. Even if, indisputably, the Schopenhauerian, metaphysical language obtrudes most of all at precisely this point, Nietzsche characterizing the individual artist as a medium through which the truly existent subject produces the artwork (III 1: 43). Let it be said only: Dionysian mimesis is not a matter of an individual artist adding art to a natural, proto-artistic Dionysian from which the artist would be distinct; rather, it is from the abysmal Dionysian circuit of transgression, disruption, reinstatement, into which the artist is cast, that the artwork is produced, nature adding art to itself in a kind of mimetic excess.

The artwork would be a mimetic double of the Dionysian. Nietzsche calls it a copy (*Abbild*), a repetition (*Wiederholung*), a recast (*Abguss*). But more telling are those designations that serve to indicate that Dionysian mimesis has nothing to do with images, much less with copies—such designations as primal resounding (*Urwiederklang*) and imageless reshining (*bildloser Wiederschein*). Indeed Nietzsche says explicitly of the Dionysian musician that he is "without any image [*ohne jedes Bild*]" (III 1: 40). Thus, the mimetic double produced in Dionysian art must be a resounding in which the Dionysian somehow announces itself, becomes manifest, yet without its manifestation occurring in and through images. In Dionysian mimesis there is—without any images—resounding excess.

Such mimesis occurs in music, as music—or, rather, in Dionysian music, which Nietzsche identifies with music as such, in distinction from the tonal architecture of Apollinian music, which can thus only be improperly called music.[22] The latter, he insists, excludes the very elements that "constitute the character of Dionysian music and thus of music as such: the emotional power of the tone, the uniform flow of the melody, and the utterly incomparable world of harmony" (III 1: 29). Nietzsche refers to the awe and terror excited by Dionysian music, and writes in a notebook entry of "the monstrous *mimetic* force of music" (III 3: 121). To a note identifying "the old dithyramb" as "purely Dionysian" (III 3: 67), *The Birth of Tragedy* adds a description of the way in which the Dionysian dithyramb incited the Greeks to the greatest exaltation of their symbolic faculties, calling into play the entire symbolism of the body in song and dance. Only as one entered into self-obliterating reunion with others and with nature could there be

22. A note extends the contrast: "Apollinian music—in rhythmic significance akin to the imagistic arts [*den bildenden Künsten*]. The revel of the mind [*Das Schwelgen des Gemüths*] was never the aim of Apollinian music, but rather the pedagogical effect. On the other hand, the orgiastic effect of music" (III 3: 72).

understanding (Nietzsche writes the word without the slightest indication of the torsion it introduces and the twisting that it would require in order to be turned toward the Dionysian): and so "the dithyrambic votary of Dionysus is understood [*wird . . . verstanden*] only by his own kind" (III 1: 29–30). Along with such exclamations, Nietzsche is careful to mark—simply yet decisively—a differentiation between Greek music, in which there was little scope for music without words, and modern music, "the infinitely richer music known and familiar to us" (III 1: 106).[23]

Nietzsche does not conceal a certain affiliation with Schopenhauer's "profound metaphysics of music" (III 1: 42). A long passage is cited from *The World as Will and Representation* to explicate the theory of music as a copy of the will. And yet, alongside the passage one might also set one of the notebook entries (from early 1871) in which music, referred to as imitation of nature, is said to be such precisely in the sense that its object (that is, what it imitates) is "the 'will,' as the most originary form of appearance" (III 3: 383). The phrase recalls quite literally the critiques of Schopenhauer's metaphysics: the posing of the will as a form of appearances, collapsing thus the fundamental distinction between will (as thing-in-itself) and appearance, marking the duplicity by use of quotation marks. Thus is marked a certain dislocation of the metaphysical language.

Yet, Dionysian art does not merely provide a musical double of the Dionysian. For all art is—to cite again the decisive indication—also a "supplement of the reality of nature placed beside it for its overcoming" (III 1: 147).[24] What, then, is the overcoming

23. Though noting this statement of differentiation, Silk and Stern seem, nonetheless, too intent on charging Nietzsche with simply patterning his account of Greek music to make it conform to modern, specifically, Wagnerian music. Even if Nietzsche can be accused of "bad scholarship," for example, for his demonstrably false "assumption that Greek music involved any kind of harmony or counterpoint comparable with those of modern music" (*Nietzsche on Tragedy*, 134), the criticism that he merely conflates Greek music with Wagner's ignores the most important and most difficult issue in Nietzsche's discourse on the rebirth of tragedy, namely, that of its difference—especially as a result of Socratism—from the original birth of tragedy from Greek music.

24. In his 1870 lectures on *Oedipus Tyrannos* Nietzsche makes the same point with respect to Dionysian art: "Thus not from the first unconditioned imitation of nature: but rather, as befits an artistic people, prudent overcoming of nature" (W 17: 301–2).

achieved by Dionysian art? How is it that the supplement not merely doubles nature but also displaces it?

In Dionysian ecstasy the limits that determine the everyday are disrupted, so that a "chasm of oblivion separates the worlds of everyday reality and of Dionysian reality." And yet, Nietzsche continues, "as soon as this everyday reality reenters consciousness, it is experienced as such with disgust [*Ekel*]; an ascetic, will-negating mood is the fruit of these states" (III 1: 52). Thus, the negativity, the danger, arises in the return from Dionysian ecstasy, in the return to the everyday, in a certain return to oneself as now in possession of the truth disclosed in ecstasy, that "true knowledge, the insight into the horrible truth." Now one sees everywhere only the horror or the absurdity of being: this is the moment of the wisdom of Silenus. It is also the moment of displacement, the moment of the supplement that constitutes the saving deed of Greek art:

Here, when the danger to his will is greatest, *art* approaches as a saving sorceress, expert at healing. She alone knows how to turn these disgusting thoughts about the horror or absurdity of existence into representations with which one can live: These are the *sublime* as the artistic taming of the horrible and the *comic* as the artistic discharge of the disgust of the absurd. The satyr chorus of the dithyramb is the saving deed of Greek art. (III 1: 53)

It will be necessary to return to this passage in the discussion of tragedy, for in the saving deed thus described one can discern already the decisive structure of tragedy and not just of Dionysian art as such.

But how, specifically, does music carry out such a saving deed? For music has, says Nietzsche, its absoluteness; that is, it does not need the image and the concept that are brought to it by poetry (III 1: 47), even if there is a certain stirring, within the spirit of music, for visual and mythical exemplification (III 1: 106). In both cases, in music as well as tragedy, it is a matter of "the joy involved in the annihilation of the individual." In the particular examples that tragedy brings forth, it presents, makes visible, the omnipotence of the will, the eternal life that continues despite all annihilation, the power and promise of rebirth. Thus, tragedy is "a translation of the instinctive, unconscious Dionysian wisdom into the language of images." Nietzsche writes in the name of tragedy: "'We believe in eternal life,' exclaims tragedy; while music is the immediate idea [*die unmittelbare Idee*] of this life." Yet, how much would one have to twist the old metaphysical words *immediate* and *idea* before they could begin to intimate how the musical double, removed and yet not removed from Dionysian truth, can by virtue of the doubling save one from the pessimistic wisdom of Silenus, drawing one on into an instinctive, unconscious Dionysian wisdom that says "yes" to the voice that cries: "Be as I am! Amidst the ceaseless flux of appearances I am the eternally creative primal mother, eternally impelling to existence, eternally finding satisfaction in this flux of appearances!" (III 1: 104).

Can it be said how the musical doubling manifests and supplements the Dionysian? Or is discourse on music intrinsically limited, consigned to endure a monstrous interval of silence? Is it perhaps only tragedy that can compensate for that silence, filling it with images?

For the Dionysian as such does not shine: "There is no Dionysian shining without an Apollinian reshining [*Wiederschein*]" (III 3: 349). The Dionysian is such that it cannot be presented as such.[25] It is not an original of which music would present images but rather is that excess that music can only let resound. It is not an origin set over against the individual who might represent it, even if as a thing-in-itself. It is nothing other than the very round of ecstasy into which one can be drawn, the circuit of transgression, disruption, reinstatement, which in its very wavering between determination and indetermination can never be *something present*. The Dionysian is an excessive figure, a figure in excess of (the) metaphysics (of presence), echoing, resounding, from beyond being.

25. For these reasons Nietzsche's thought in *The Birth of Tragedy* is not so easily caught in the trap of logocentrism as Bernard Pautrat supposes, at least at one level of his very remarkable reading. Nietzsche does not simply put music (voice) in place of logos, otherwise maintaining the structure intact and thus remaining within a melocentrism that would be only the other name of logocentrism (Bernard Pautrat, *Versions du soleil: Figures et système de Nietzsche* [Paris: Éditions du Seuil, 1971], 68–73). For what music makes manifest in Dionysian mimesis is precisely such that it cannot be reduced to presence, cannot be presented to and by a logos become melos.

3 | T R A G E D Y —

Sublime Ecstasy

a

The Birth of Tragedy leads to the threshold. Nietzsche's final words, an invitation, are spoken by an old Athenian: "But now follow me to the tragedy and sacrifice with me in the temple of both gods!" (III 1: 152).

Imagine the site: "Everything was assembled to accord with devotion: the wide circle of 20,000 spectators, the blue sky above, the chorus coming forward with golden wreaths and fine garments, the architecturally beautiful scene, the union of musical, poetic, and mimetic art" (W 17: 303).

Incipit tragoedia. Oedipus steps forth from his palace and exhorts the young generation stemming from old Cadmus, the *neu Geschlecht*, in Hölderlin's translation.[1] The word names in its full extent the natural order for the violation of which Oedipus is to suffer, the natural order of generation that has indeed already been violated when the tragedy begins.

Stepping forth, he speaks as befits the king he is:

I Oedipus whom all men call the great [κλεινός]

(OT 8)

Oedipus is renowned, above all, for his wisdom. Whether his own or the gift of a god, that wisdom enabled him to solve the riddle of the sphinx and thus to save the city of Thebes. And yet, in spite of his wisdom, he is destined to the utmost errancy, misery, wretchedness. At that moment when Jocasta comes to behold in all

---

1. *Die Trauerspiele des Sophokles,* translated by Friedrich Hölderlin (Frankfurt am Main: Friedrich Wilmans, 1804), 1:3. English translations are adapted primarily from those by David Grene (*Oedipus Tyrannos*) and Robert Fitzgerald (*Oedipus at Colonus*) in *Greek Tragedies,* ed. David Grene and Richmond Lattimore, vols. 1, 3. I have used the Greek texts in Sophokles, *Dramen* (Munich: Artemis Verlag, 1985) and have consulted the German translation by Wilhelm Willige included in this volume.

its horror the destiny that has drawn her into an errancy from which only death may disentangle her, at that moment when she is about to rush away in wild grief to take her own life, she addresses Oedipus, addresses him finally in truth:

> O Oedipus, wretched [δύστηνε] Oedipus!
> That is all I can call you, and the last thing
> That I shall ever call you.
>
> (OT 1071–72)

Oedipus is to suffer. Even though the deeds for which he is to suffer are themselves deeds more suffered than done (OC 265–67), miseries born involuntarily (OC 963), a destiny drawn under utmost concealment, a destiny withdrawn even from the vision of wise Oedipus, a destiny that remained withdrawn, under concealment, until all were ensnared by the errancy it had produced and Thebes was thus polluted by the very one who had once saved the city.

Oedipus is to undergo, in Nietzsche's words, monstrous suffering (*ungeheures Leiden*) (III 1: 61). His suffering is linked to monstrosity, to divergence from nature within nature, to violation of the natural order in the very course of nature, to violation of the order of *Geschlecht,* which orders and delimits individuals within families and generations. The old blind prophet Teiresias—whose very wisdom is linked to confusion of *Geschlechter*—is the first to speak of the concealed monstrosity, of Oedipus's blindness to the monstrosity in which he is entangled and which he has, if unwittingly, produced—

> Establishing a grim equality
> Between you and your children.
>
> (OT 425)

Only much later, after a double exchange between vision and blindness has brought the aged Oedipus in view of his destiny, only then can he tell truly (ὀρθόν) of what he has suffered: that his beloved daughters were given birth by the very one who gave birth to himself, that they are both his daughters and his sisters, their father's sisters (OC 513–18, 532–35). Only at the distance of a messenger's report can it be told how Jocasta, finally seeing all, raged against the monstrosity of a mother producing children by her own son:

And then she groaned and cursed the bed in which
She brought forth husband by her husband, children
By her own child, a wretched doubling [δύστηνος διπλοῦς].

(OT 1248–50)

It is a destiny woven by doubling, by a duplicity that unites what the order of *Geschlecht* would keep distinct: husband and son, wife and mother, parent and child. It is a destiny through which one and the same individual—wretched Oedipus—doubles as both husband and son of another—unfortunate Jocasta—drawn thus into doubling as both wife and mother. The lines of the generations are crossed, the linearity of generation interrupted, primarily by Oedipus's incest, but also by the connection of his patricide to incest: instead of the father living on in the son who would extend his line into a new generation, Oedipus, by killing his father, can become both son and father, crossing the lines. The doubling has the effect of exceeding the limits that determine the generational order of individuals, transgressing and disrupting those limits while, as the very condition of the disruptive transgression, reinstating that order, leaving it intact in the very production of indeterminacy. Monstrosity as indeterminate dyad. Also, of course, as the Dionysian.

Such is the errancy, the Dionysian excess, from which Oedipus must suffer in spite of his wisdom. Or rather, as Nietzsche insists, *because of* his wisdom, that wisdom that has the power to compel nature to yield its secrets:

It is this knowledge that I find expressed in that horrible triad of Oedipus's destinies: the same man who solves the riddle of nature—that double-specied [*doppelgearteten*] Sphinx—must also break the most sacred natural orders by murdering his father and marrying his mother. (III 1: 63)

The wisdom of Oedipus with its power over the cross-bred Sphinx is itself something monstrous. Or rather, as Teiresias says in the very beginning of his very first speech: Oedipus's wisdom is *terrible* (δεινόν) (OT 315). For it is a wisdom that proves to be its own undoing, revealing finally the destiny woven in concealment; it is a wisdom that reveals its very unwisdom, its submission to concealment, its blindness. The same is said of the sight of Oedipus blinding himself, stabbing Jocasta's golden brooches into his own eyeballs, striking his eyes again and again until a black rain and bloody hail poured down: what happened was *terrible* to see (OT 1267).

The tragedy is gathered in the great choral song that just precedes the report of Jocasta's suicide and of Oedipus's blinding himself. The chorus sings to the generations of men, to the *Geschlechter der Sterblichen*, in Hölderlin's translation. It proclaims a wisdom that is terrible, almost as terrible as the wisdom of Silenus that declares it best not to have lived at all: mortals (βροτοί) are counted as equal with those who do not live at all. There is no difference that is not mere seeming, neither between the generations nor even between living and not-living. Only the appearance of happiness, of good fortune (εὐδαιμονία), turning all too soon into something worse, into decline and turning away (ἀποκλίνω). As with wretched Oedipus and his destiny, his *Dämon,* as Hölderlin translates—or rather, transliterates—the Greek δαίμων.

Listen to the beginning of the wild, haunting song:

> O generations of men, how I
> Count you as equal with those who live
> Not at all!
> For who, what man wins more
> Of happiness than a seeming
> And after that a turning away?
> Oedipus, you are my pattern of this,
> You and your destiny!
> Wretched Oedipus, whom of all men
> I do not at all call happy.
>
> (OT 1186–96)

In *Oedipus at Colonus* another tone prevails. Though the old man is abandoned to his suffering, something else descends upon him as if from the gods: in *The Birth of Tragedy* Nietzsche calls it a superterrestrial cheerfulness (*überirdische Heiterkeit*), an infinite transfiguration (*unendliche Verklärung*) (III 1: 62). In the lectures on *Oedipus Tyrannos* he calls it σωφροσύνη: it is a matter of the most profound submission (*tiefste Ergebung*) and resignation in the face of the immeasurable distance separating the human from the godly (W 17: 321). Finally Oedipus comes to bear the separation; in the end he no longer suffers from it. Though, otherwise, separation can only engender suffering, Dionysian suffering as dismemberment, separation from self, loss of self. The aged Oedipus has passed through such loss, such separation; he has suffered so monstrously from it that finally his suffering is transfigured, not by virtue of any action but through the most profound submission; or rather, as Nietzsche formulates it, Oedipus achieves his highest activity precisely in his purely passive comportment (III 1: 62).

At the end of *Oedipus Tyrannos,* when self-blinded Oedipus speaks finally to Antigone and Ismene, he broaches the separation that he must suffer, through which he must suffer, must pass, the separation that would set apart what had been monstrously united by double-crossing destiny. He sets apart, within himself, brother and father:

> O children,
> Where are you? Come here, come to my hands,
> A brother's hands which turned your father's eyes,
> Those bright eyes you knew once, to what you now see,
> A father seeing nothing, knowing nothing,
> Begetting you from his own source of life.
>
> (OT 1480–85)

When *Oedipus at Colonus* begins, separation has indeed been extended almost without limit. Oedipus has been driven from Thebes, estranged once and for all from his sons, and for many years he has wandered from city to city. Only his daughters remain with him, Antigone, who must guide him, and Ismene, who comes not only to bring news of the treacheries in Thebes but also to intimate to her father a reversal:

> For the gods who threw you down sustain you now.
>
> (OC 394)

But then, finally, old blind Oedipus no longer needs to be led. A messenger reports

> how he
> Left this place with no friend leading him,
> Acting, himself, as guide for all of us.
>
> (OC 1587–89)

In the end, Oedipus himself leads the way to the place where he is to die. In the end, there is separation without limit, as in death, purifying the horrible unification of husband and son, of father and brother, that had been his destiny.

Thus Hölderlin reads the great Sophoclean tragedies: "The presentation of the tragic rests above all on conceiving the monstrous—as god and man are coupled and as natural force and man's innermost limitlessly unite in rage—in such a way that limitless unification is purified through limitless separation."[2]

Yet, if separation purifies, it does so by transfiguring. For it is not a matter of sin and guilt; though his action set in motion a violation of nature that could not but produce a dissolution of nature within himself, Oedipus insists that in murdering Laius he was unknowing (ἄϊδϱις) (OC 548). His errancy leads to dissolution and suffering; and yet, says Nietzsche, "through his monstrous suffering he spreads a magical power of blessing that remains effective even beyond his decease." In the end, "his action also produces a higher magical circle of effects which found a new world on the ruins of the old one that has been overthrown" (III 1: 61).

Long before Theseus arrives on the scene, Oedipus announces that he brings advantage to the Athenians. When the king arrives, Oedipus tells him:

> I come to give you something, and the gift
> Is my own beaten self.
>
> (OC 576–77)

The gift must wait until Oedipus is at the point of death and burial; it is implicated in that burial, which proves in a sense not to take place at all. At the place where he is to die, Oedipus will give Theseus the blessing that he has promised:

> I shall disclose to you, O son of Aegeus,
> What is appointed for you and for your city:
> A thing that age will never wear away.
> Presently now, without anyone to guide me,
> I'll lead you to the place where I must die.
>
> (OC 1518–21)

At the moment of final, limitless separation, at the moment of death, Oedipus's suffering is transfigured into an outpouring of a magical power of blessing: a new world founded on the ruins of the

---

2. Hölderlin, "Anmerkungen zum Oedipus," in *Die Trauerspiele des Sophokles*, 1:107.

old. From life to death, from death to life: a good crossing is to be made by Oedipus.

It is of this crossing that the chorus sings in the last great song of *Oedipus at Colonus*. In the face of the horror of death, looking into the eyes of Persephone, Hades, and Cerberus, the chorus prays that Oedipus may have a good crossing, that his crossing may be clear, free, open (καθαρός):

> If it is right for me to worship
> The invisible goddess
> And pray to the master plunged in night,
> Hades, Hades;
> Let not our friend come to his end in weariness and grief,
> Down to his fate all-concealed,
> The burial plain, the Stygian abode.
> Because his sufferings were great and unmerited,
> It is fitting that some just daimon relieve him.
>
> O gods under the earth, and tameless
> Beast lying in the cavern,
> Howling at the gates visited by many guests,
> Hades's guard forever, it is said.
> I pray you, offspring of Earth and Tartarus,
> To let the descent be clear
> As Oedipus goes down to the underworld
> On that burial plain that living men fear.
> I call on you to grant Oedipus eternal sleep.
>
> (OC 1556–78)

His daughters are, finally, assured that his end was free and blessed. And the messenger who reports his passing declares that

> he was taken without lamentation,
> Illness or suffering; indeed his end
> Was wonderful if mortal's ever was.
>
> (OC 1664–66)

b

While these great choral songs still echo, one will hesitate to pose to tragedy the philosophical question, the Socratic question (τί ἐστι . . .?), anticipating the opposition that Nietzsche will expose between the tragic and the Socratic. If tragedy cannot be simply submitted to the Socratic question without one's thereby taking sides with Socrates, taking sides within the opposition against tragedy and to this extent turning away from what would be sung in it, then the question will have to be also unsaid from the moment it is posed. A certain writing under erasure is thus required when Nietzsche's text addresses the question of the essence of tragedy (*das Wesen der Tragödie*) (III 1: 91) or of the properly tragic (*das eigentlich Tragische*) (III 1: 138); that is, the operation of erasure needs to be brought openly into play in the reinscription of Nietzsche's text.

It can indeed be said that tragedy is not what the aestheticians say it is: it is neither, says Nietzsche, "the struggle of the hero with fate" (Oedipus's suffering through separation is hardly to be called struggle) nor "the triumph of the moral world order" (even if it were a matter of triumph, the order at issue in the case of Oedipus is the order of *Geschlecht,* not of morality); nor is tragedy simply the discharge of the emotions, the catharsis of Aristotle, "of which philologists are not sure whether it should be included among medical or moral phenomena" (III 1: 138). It is, rather, to be said, as of art in general, that tragedy is a supplement. Or, rather, it is not quite, not simply, to be said, for what Nietzsche writes, holding the assertion in a certain suspension, is: "That life is really so tragic would least of all explain the origin of an art form; if indeed [provided—*wenn anders*] art is not merely imitation of the reality of nature but rather a metaphysical supplement of the reality of nature, placed beside it for its overcoming" (III 1: 147). Let it be said, then, in the same way—that is, also unsaid—that tragedy is a mimetic supplement of the reality of nature.

The mimetic character of tragedy is rooted, though not exclusively, in the mimetic character of the music from which it is born. Following Schopenhauer, Nietzsche insists on a fundamental differentiation between music and the imagistic (*bildliche*) arts; inasmuch as this differentiation reproduces that between Dionysian and Apollinian, he even credits Schopenhauer with having recognized the "monstrous opposition" between the latter, even without the clue provided by the symbolism of the Hellenic gods. Nietzsche cites a long passage that identifies music as a copy of the will itself, in contrast to the imagistic arts, which produce copies of phenomena.[3] He refers also to the further development given to this differentiation by Wagner: because music does not imitate phenomena, it cannot be understood and evaluated according to the concept of beauty (as phenomenal form capable of arousing delight) (III 1: 99–100).[4] Nietzsche does not mention explicitly the corollary drawn by Wagner: that music can be understood and evaluated only according to the category of the sublime (RW 9: 56).

Here, faced with this most massive and literal reinscription of Schopenhauer, one needs to let come again into play that dislocation of the Schopenhauerian thing-in-itself that was traced in the above discussion of Dionysian art (chap. 2 d). Then it would not be a matter of music's imitating "the inner contradiction of the will with itself" (WWV 1: §52)—this phrase itself already introducing the dislocating effect. Or, rather, it *would* be a matter of imitating this contradiction *but only as* extended to such a degree that it could no longer be thought *within* the will-in-itself but only as that contradiction that is both more and less than contradiction—that is, as the movement of Dionysian truth, of the abyss into which one enters in that movement of excess. Music would be the imageless manifestation of the Dionysian abyss, of the abysmal figure of ecstasy.

The most decisive development in Greek art is the crossing of such Dionysian mimesis with a certain Apollinian mimesis. In and through this crossing Apollinian images come to reflect music and the Dionysian abyss manifest therein. It is this crossing that opens and structures the space of tragedy.

3. One cannot but notice that despite Nietzsche's enthusiasm for Schopenhauer's "profound metaphysics of music" (III 1: 42) he is virtually silent about Schopenhauer's theory of tragedy. Later, in the "Attempt at a Self-Critique," he makes it abundantly clear that Schopenhauer's view could hardly be more at variance with what is said of tragedy in *The Birth of Tragedy*. In the later text he poses the question: "What, after all, did Schopenhauer think of tragedy?" Then he cites from *The World as Will and Representation:* "That which bestows on everything tragic its peculiar elevating force is the emergence of the knowledge that the world, that life, cannot give real satisfaction and hence is *not worthy* of our affection: this constitutes the tragic spirit—it leads to *resignation*" (III 1: 14).

4. From the notebooks: "Beauty is something that plays no part whatsoever in the field of music" (III 3: 75); "Music struck [*herausgeschlagen*] from a tragic matter—no longer the beautiful but the world is explained: thus from music arises the tragic conception, which contradicts beauty" (III 3: 72).

The new germ that was to develop into the dithyramb and, finally, into tragedy first appears in Greek lyric poetry. In a passage already cited in part in the above discussion of Dionysian art, Nietzsche describes the supervening of the Apollinian upon Dionysian music:

First of all, as a Dionysian artist he has become completely one with the primal one, its pain and contradiction, and he produces the copy of this primal one as music, assuming that music has been correctly termed a repetition and a recast of the world; now, however, under the Apollinian dream inspiration, this music becomes visible to him again as in a symbolic dream-image. That imageless and ungraspable reshining [*Jener bild- und begrifflose Wiederschein*] of primal pain in music, with its redemption in shining, now produces a second mirroring as a specific symbol or example. (III 1: 39–40)

So, in lyric poetry the music produced by Dionysian mimesis becomes visible to the artist in images; it is made visible in the images evoked by the poem. Hence, to the imageless Dionysian reverberation (*Urwiederklang*) there is added an image, an Apollinian shining in images. More precisely, the image—as symbol, as example—is generated from out of the music; it is the becoming-visible of the music. Thus Nietzsche writes of Dionysus or the Dionysian reveler sunk in slumber on the high mountain pastures in the noonday sun—as depicted in *The Bacchae:* "and now Apollo approaches him and touches him with the laurel. Then the Dionysian-musical enchantment of the sleeper emits, as it were, image sparks, lyric poems, which in their highest development are called tragedies and dramatic dithyrambs" (III 1: 40). In contrast to the distance at which the Apollinian artist takes joyous satisfaction in images, there is virtually no separation between the lyrist and his images, which are only projections of himself; hence the apparent subjectivity of lyric poetry (which, Nietzsche notes, misled Schopenhauer into considering lyric poetry as a mingling of what amount to aesthetic and unaesthetic states). It is decisive, however, that the self of the lyrist, coinciding with his images, is a self that is already lost to Dionysian ecstasy, a self that "has already surrendered his subjectivity in the Dionysian process" (III 1: 40). The lyrist is not an individual projecting his own subjectivity into poetic images, but rather one who is outside himself, exceeding the limits of any individuality.

Nietzsche extends this account to the folk song, calling it a *perpetuum vestigium* of the union of Apollinian and Dionysian:

First of all, however, we must regard the folk song as the musical mirror of the world, as the original melody, which seeks for itself a parallel dream phenomenon and expresses it in poetry. *Melody is therefore primary and universal* and so may admit of several objectifications in several texts. . . . Out of itself melody gives birth to the poem ever anew; that is what the strophic form of the folk song signifies. (III 1: 44–45)

Nietzsche refers to the way that *Des Knaben Wunderhorn* scatters image sparks all around. The folk song is indicative of the relation between poetry and music, "the only possible relation," Nietzsche calls it. One sees in the folk song how language is strained to the utmost that it might "imitate music [*die Musik nachzuahmen*]" (III 1: 45). Music does not imitate the images called up in the language of poetry; in Schopenhauer's terms, music does not imitate phenomena. Rather, conversely, the images imitate music, present an example (an analogous example or expression, Schopenhauer and Nietzsche call it) that mirrors the musical manifestation of something unpresentable, withdrawn from presence. Nietzsche refers to the example of Beethoven's "pastoral" symphony: it is not a matter of imitating in music the "scene by the brook" or the "merry gathering of rustics," but rather of a discharge of music in images (III 1: 45–46). The directionality of the mimesis is irreversibly fixed.

Nietzsche turns more directly to the question of language. Because language is "the organ and symbol of phenomena," it can never "disclose the innermost depth of music"; for, says Nietzsche, again reinscribing Schopenhauer, music is related "to the primal contradiction and primal pain in the heart of the primal one," hence, to "a sphere that is beyond and prior to all phenomena" (III 1: 47).[5] Insofar as music is mimesis of the primal one beyond all

5. In one of the notebook entries discussed above (chap. 2 c), in which Nietzsche disrupts Schopenhauer's dualism and declares the will "nothing but the most general form of appearance," he goes on to develop the question of language along lines that no longer depend on simple correlation with phenomena in distinction from the primal one. He proposes that in nature there is a paradigm for the union of poetry and music, namely, in the "doubleness in the essence of language." The sphere of language corresponding to appearing will—will as a form of appearance—is the *tone* of speech, in distinction from what he calls the *Geberdensymbolik*, which includes the entire sphere of consonants and vowels. He

phenomena, there are definite—and, one would think, narrow—limits to any discourse on music.[6] Perhaps even any discourse that would venture beyond the surface of music, beyond its formal structure and sensible quality, would have to be retracted, if indeed the thing-in-itself is as unspeakable as it would seem. What would pass for discourse on the meaning of music would, then, always have fallen into the trap in which the young Nietzsche found Schopenhauer to be so thoroughly caught, the trap that consists in inadvertently transferring to the thing-in-itself attributes derived simply from the opposition to appearances. If, on the other hand, the dislocation of the primal one is brought into play, tuning music to the abysmal movement of indeterminacy, to the figure of ecstasy, the trap will be different but no less threatening. Though in a different way, the effect will be still that of installing a region—or, better, an operation—of silence in Nietzsche's discourse on music.

In its highest development the crossing of Apollinian and Dionysian takes the form of tragedy. Like lyric poetry, tragedy has a double mimetic structure, pairing an Apollinian mimesis and a

---

speculates that the tonal ground of language may be common to all languages. Yet, while, on the one hand, he draws the will back into the compass of a certain part of language, namely, the tonal ground, on the other hand, he also refers to something "utterly inscrutable to us," something of which the will would be the appearance, something that to this extent would still be withheld from language (III 3: 378–79).

Still another line of development is broached in the incipient genealogy of the text "On Truth and Lies in a Nonmoral Sense." Here even the relation of language to phenomena (that is, things as related to man in certain socially conditioned ways) is taken to be disrupted by a double metaphorical operation: "The 'thing in itself' . . . is likewise something quite incomprehensible to the creator of language and something not in the least worth striving for. This creator only designates the relations of things to men, and for expressing these relations he lays hold of the boldest metaphors. To begin with, a nerve stimulus is transferred into an image: first metaphor. The image, in turn, is imitated in a sound: second metaphor. And each time there is a complete overleaping of one sphere, right into the middle of an entirely new and different one" (III 2: 373).

6. Schopenhauer also insists on such limits, as limits of the concept and not specifically of language. Referring to music, he says: "Even in the explanation of this wonderful art, the concept shows its inadequacy and its limits." It is necessary to refer to such limits in interpreting Schopenhauer's subsequent remark that a perfect and complete explanation of music, thus a repetition in concepts of what music expresses, would be a sufficient explanation of the world in concepts, that is, the true philosophy (WWV 1: §52).

Dionysian mimesis. Yet, in the development of tragedy the Apollinian image ceases to be evoked merely in phantasy through the poetic word and comes, eventually, to be visibly present as the scene produced on the proscenium. On the other side, the poet in his capacity as first of all a Dionysian artist is replaced by the chorus. Thus is opened between scene and chorus, between proscenium and orchestra, the space of tragedy.

The double mimesis that structures this space is repeatedly outlined in the course of *The Birth of Tragedy*. No less than in the lyric and the folk song, the directionality of the mimetic complex is irreversibly fixed, the images, the scene pictured or actually presented on stage, being generated from the choral song, born from the musical womb:

We must understand Greek tragedy as the Dionysian chorus that ever anew discharges itself in an Apollinian world of images. Thus the choral parts with which tragedy is interlaced are, as it were, the womb that gave birth to the whole of the so-called dialogue, that is, the entire world of the stage, the genuine drama. In several successive discharges this primal ground of tragedy radiates this vision of the drama. (III 1: 58)

The structure is again outlined in a passage in which Nietzsche ventures to write—in a way that would require reinscription under erasure—of "the essence [*Wesen*] of tragedy," describing it as "a manifestation and imaging [*Verbildlichung*] of Dionysian states, as the visible symbolizing of music, as the dream-world of a Dionysian rapture" (III 1: 91). Thus, the choral parts generate the scene, casting forth the images on stage rather than simply reflecting in song the events pictured there. It is for this reason that tragedy is *gathered* (thus I translate the early Greek λέγειν) in the great choral songs. And it is because of this gathering, not because they are vocal or linguistic, that these songs bespeak the λόγος. For instance, those that proclaim the terrible wisdom of the Dionysian, and those that pray for a good crossing to the underworld, for a death that would be, if mortal's ever was, wonderful.

Thus can Nietzsche understand what is proclaimed unequivocally by the tradition: that the chorus is the origin of tragedy, that tragedy arose from the chorus and was in the beginning nothing but chorus. In that beginning tragedy was still somewhat like lyric poetry: its Apollinian vision was merely evoked in dramatic phantasy, generated through the dance, tone, and words of the chorus.

The entire space of tragedy was opened beginning from the chorus and in the beginning was extended beyond the choral womb only through dramatic phantasy, that is, it was opened as such only through such choral phantasy.[7] Only later was the vision, the scene, actually presented on stage and the space of tragedy actually bounded by the proscenium.

Whether or not it is actually presented on stage, the scene is an image produced in, operating within, an Apollinian mimesis. In these Apollinian images the Dionysian chorus is itself imaged; in its vision the chorus sees itself cast forth in the images that eventually come to be actually presented on stage. Thus it is that the stage hero is none other than Dionysus himself, originally present only to the dramatic phantasy of the chorus, later stepping out onto the stage like a colossus (III 2: 15). Indeed, Dionysus is the *only* hero to come onto the stage of Greek tragedy—that is, all the others are only masks of Dionysus:

The tradition is undisputed that Greek tragedy in its earliest form had for its sole theme the sufferings of Dionysus and that for a long time the only stage hero was Dionysus himself. But it may be claimed with equal certainty that until Euripides, Dionysus never ceased to be the tragic hero; that all the celebrated figures of the Greek stage—Prometheus, Oedipus, etc.—are mere masks of this original hero, Dionysus. (III 1: 67)

In the case of Oedipus the countenance of the original hero is deeply engraved on the mask: in the figure of monstrosity, in the look of terrible wisdom, in the signs of separation and of suffering.

The chorus can give birth to tragedy, to the scene, only by being the site of another mimesis, a Dionysian mimesis. Nietzsche calls it the primal dramatic phenomenon (*das dramatische Urphänomen*): "to see oneself transformed before one's own eyes and then to act as if one had actually entered into another body, another character." In this phenomenon there is "a surrendering of individuality by entering into an alien nature," as in the case of an actor who sees

7. From the notebooks (1870–72): "In the origin of tragedy only the chorus, in the orchestra, is real, while the world of the stage, the persons and events on it, were visible only as living images, as the shining forms of the Apollinian phantasy of the chorus" (III 3: 199). "The drama as at first a vision of the chorus" (III 3: 233). "Ancient tragedy: the chorus that dreamed an Apollinian dream" (III 3: 319). "the chorus, which has a vision and, enraptured, describes what it beholds!" (III 3: 289).

before him the role, the very character, that he is to play. The primal dramatic phenomenon thus consists in being outside oneself, exceeding the limits of one's individuality, disrupting thereby the order and the lines of family, tradition, and city: "The dithyrambic chorus is a chorus of transformed characters whose civic past and social status have been totally forgotten" (III 1: 57). The primal dramatic phenomenon is, in a word, ecstasy.

Even though the chorus is the primary site of this phenomenon, it also occurs on the side of the spectators—indeed to such an extent as to efface the very opposition between the spectators and the chorus whose resounding songs could not but draw those spectators into the very ecstasy that they celebrate: "there was at bottom no opposition between public and chorus: everything is merely a great sublime chorus of dancing and singing satyrs or of those who permit themselves to be represented by such satyrs" (III 1: 55; cf. III 3: 285–86). The outcome is Dionysian mimesis: "this is the most immediate effect of the Dionysian tragedy, that the state and society and, quite generally, the gulfs between man and man give way to an overwhelming feeling of unity leading back to the very heart of nature" (III 1: 52). The outcome is an artistic doubling of that very movement of excess, of ecstatic truth, into which the dancing and singing chorus must have entered, a doubling that would produce, not a detached image of a natural original, but only a resounding of an abyss.

Granted the double mimetic structure, can it, in the end, still be said—as Nietzsche himself says in the opening paragraph of *The Birth of Tragedy*—that tragedy is equally Apollinian and Dionysian? Does Apollinian vision, even if generated from the choral womb, remain, in the end, coordinate with Dionysian music? Or is their coupling such that the latter comes finally to predominate?

A certain coordination is suggested by Nietzsche's term *fraternal bond (Bruderbund)*, though one cannot but contrast such coordination with the sexual pairing proposed in Nietzsche's initial statement. The coordination lies in the way that in tragedy each is bound to the other and its character determined by the other. The Dionysian is lent a certain visibility in the Apollinian image projected on stage, and the Apollinian is made to image, not just the everyday, but the Dionysian ecstasy in which the everyday is exceeded:

Thus the difficult relation of the Apollinian and the Dionysian in tragedy may really be symbolized by a fraternal union of the two gods: Dionysus speaks the language of Apollo, but Apollo finally the language of Dionysus: and so the highest goal of tragedy and of art as such is attained. (III 1: 135–36; cf. III 2: 48)

And yet, there can be no doubt but that tragedy surpasses the Apollinian: Apollo speaks *finally* the language of Dionysus. Nietzsche says of tragedy that it "attains as a whole an effect that lies *beyond all Apollinian artistic effects*." And thus: "In the total effect [*Gesammtwirkung*] of tragedy, the Dionysian predominates once again" (III 1: 135). It predominates because what the tragedy imitates as a whole—in its "total effect"—is the Dionysian. Even its Apollinian images are images of Dionysus, and to this extent it is, in the end, a double mimesis of the Dionysian.

But what is the total effect of tragedy? What is the effect of the tragic mimesis of the Dionysian? What does tragedy effect beyond the mere production of musical and poetic doubles of the Dionysian? What does it effect beyond the double imitation?—"if indeed art is not merely imitation of the reality of nature but rather a metaphysical supplement of the reality of nature, placed beside it for its overcoming" (III 1: 147)?

C

How, then, is tragedy a supplement? How does the imitation that it places beside the Dionysian abyss effect an overcoming of that abyss? How does tragedy, as supplement, thus bring about a displacement and replacement of the abyss that the Dionysian opens within nature? Does overcoming the abyss require closing it off, leaving it sealed and forgotten like an abandoned mine or cave? Or does one come, in the moment of tragedy, to be suspended over the abyss? Does one come to stand, trembling, at its edge?

These questions move closer to that which in reinscription under erasure might be called the essence of tragedy. And yet, it is not only a matter of crossing out (cancelling while also leaving in play) the metaphysical determinations from which Nietzsche's text has begun to twist free, of enforcing that freedom by a way of writing—that is, stylistically. It is also a matter of attending to the tension between tragic drama and the theoretical attitude, the tension that—even before those determinations from which Nietzsche's text would twist free—draws tragedy away from the vision of θεωρία, withdraws it from the theoretical demand for final transparency. A theoretical account of tragedy—one that would contribute to aesthetic science—will encounter limits, points beyond which the phenomenon itself precludes transparency and resists accounting—or, rather, a theoretical account will *not* encounter such limits, *if* to encounter means to come upon something firmly, determinately established, which would be already to violate the very operation of such limits. One cannot even fix the point beyond which—nonetheless—tragedy, the disclosure accomplished in it, can only be acknowledged. Finally, as at the end of *The Birth of Tragedy,* one must submit oneself to tragedy and follow the old Athenian off to the temple.

Bringing forth a mimetic double of nature, tragedy would, through that double, disclose nature; or, rather, it would disclose that divergence from nature within nature that constitutes monstrosity. Such disclosure is, however, anything but the mere production of a duplicate that would simply present nature more transparently and more closely at hand. For Dionysian monstrosity can never be simply presented; it is nothing presentable. Neither could mere duplication, even if it were possible, ever effect an overcoming.

It is disclosure that is at issue even in that way of expressing the effect of tragedy that Nietzsche will later reject in the interest of laughter: the effect of tragedy, the overcoming that it effects, he describes as the production of metaphysical comfort (*Trost*). Thrown beyond the everyday, oblivious to self, the Dionysian reveler gazes into the terrible destructiveness of the abyss. The danger comes when such a one returns to the everyday: thrown back upon oneself yet aware of the abysmal truth once seen, one now sees everywhere—beneath everything—only the horror or absurdity of existence. The danger is pessimism, the onset of the wisdom of Silenus.

This pessimism, this threat brought on by exposure to the Dionysian abyss, is what is overcome by tragedy.[8] One could say,

8. From the notebooks: "Tragedy is the natural healing power against the Dionysian" (III 3: 69).

then, that tragedy provides the means whereby a good crossing can be made, back from the Dionysian to the everyday, a crossing like that made by Er, back from Hades, identified by Heraclitus with Dionysus. A question appears on the horizon, the question whether philosophy is a means for such a crossing, whether it too can lead one safely back, or even whether it alone can truly lead one back into the city.

The disclosure achieved in tragedy leads one back in an overcoming that leaves one comforted. The course of this return is traced in a passage already cited, which now I reinscribe: tragedy alone knows how to turn these disgusting thoughts about the horror of existence into representations with which one can live: the *sublime* as the artistic taming of the horrible. Let it be said, then, that tragedy exposes one to the abyss, disclosing the abyss by way of a double mimesis; *and yet,* that tragedy, in its very disclosure of the abyss, protects, saves, even heals one from the destructive consequences that such exposure can have. Tragedy leads one back, leaves one finally comforted, by letting the horrible turn into the sublime. Exposing one mimetically to the abyss, tragedy at the same time lets the abyss be displaced, lets it be replaced with the sublime. As a mimetic supplement, tragedy is a *disclosing of the abyss as sublime.* Let it not go unremarked that such disclosure, precisely because it is abysmal, cannot but recoil upon the *is,* crossing it out even if still letting it remain legible. As tragedy, too, crosses out what it discloses, letting it nonetheless remain: displaced and replaced.

In the end, then, it is a matter of the sublime. Indeed, it is quite remarkable how frequently and decisively Nietzsche refers to the sublime in *The Birth of Tragedy.* Though there may be a few instances where the term is used loosely or in ways that do not entirely cohere with the determination of tragedy (perhaps most notably his reference to Homer as sublime [III 1: 33]) or where it is used in a quite different connection (for example, his description of the metaphysical illusion accompanying science as sublime [III 1: 95]), most of the references cohere with the determination or even expand it in a certain direction: thus Nietzsche refers to Wagner as his sublime predecessor (III 1: 20); he refers to the sublime art of Attic tragedy (III 1: 38); he describes the sublime satisfaction with which Dionysian man rests his eyes on the satyr (III 1: 54); and he refers to the sublime gesture by which Apollo redeems the world of suffering (III 1: 35), sublime inasmuch as it prefigures Apollo's role in tragedy.

In the crucial position given the sublime in this determination of tragedy, Nietzsche extends the Wagnerian position already endorsed, the position that insists on the inappropriateness of the concept of beauty for understanding music. Now much the same is to be said of tragedy, at least considered in its total effect. And now, again following Wagner, Nietzsche brings forth the concept of the sublime as that which befits Dionysian art.[9]

Schopenhauer is to some extent in the background of this shift to the sublime, for it was his differentiation of music from the other arts that provided the framework for Wagner's redistribution of the arts with respect to the beautiful and the sublime. And yet, for Schopenhauer tragedy does not lie on the side of music but rather, as the culmination of poetry, belongs among those arts that, objectifying the world by means of ideas, are to be fundamentally differentiated from music (WWV 1: §§51–52). Furthermore, Schopenhauer interprets both the beautiful and the sublime as means by which one can rise to pure contemplation of ideas, becoming thus for a brief span a will-less subject of knowing. The difference would lie only in the fact that with the beautiful, pure knowledge is gained without struggle, whereas in the case of the sublime, the beholder must first tear himself away from certain objects, hostile in their might or greatness, and only then can attain that contemplation attained immediately by way of the beautiful. Schopenhauer concludes that the feeling of the sublime "in its principal determination [*in der Hauptbestimmung*] is the same as the feeling of the beautiful"; thus, he concludes, "there result several degrees of the sublime, in fact transitions from the beautiful to the sublime" (WWV 1: §39).

It should be noted, first of all, how thoroughly Schopenhauer reduces the very difference on which Wagner and, following him, Nietzsche would base the fundamental differentiation between the imagistic arts, on the one hand, and music and tragedy, on the

9. One of the notebook entries associates the beautiful with the dream and with measure, in the way already familiar from the discussions of the Apollinian in the opening sections of *The Birth of Tragedy*. But the note also associates the sublime with rapture (*Rausch*) and with excess, thus linking the sublime to the Dionysian as closely as beauty is linked to the Apollinian (III 3: 157).

other. The difference between the beautiful and the sublime becomes, with Schopenhauer, an indifferent one, to be bridged by a series of examples. To say nothing of how he has levelled out a difference, dulled an opposition, that for Kant was so monstrous that it not only threatened the coherence of the entire critique of aesthetic judgment but also, within that critique, had to be thought by reference to such fundamental differences as that between sensible and intelligible, understanding and reason. For Kant the sublime is something unlimitedly great or powerful, something that, contrary to Schopenhauer, does not actually threaten the one who beholds it but rather overwhelms, exceeds, the imaginative powers so as to draw one up toward a universal destination. But whatever may be the outcome—whether pure contemplation, as in Schopenhauer, or such moral reflection as Schopenhauer would completely exclude from this sphere—the movement into which one is thrown initially by the sublime is no indifferent struggle that, however violent, would leave the sublime essentially continuous with the beautiful. Rather, as Kant describes it:

This movement can (especially in its beginning) be compared to a tremoring [*Erschütterung*], that is, to a rapidly alternating repulsion from and attraction to the same object. That which is excessive [*das Überschwengliche*] for the imagination (up to which it is impelled in the apprehension of intuition) is, as it were, an abyss [*Abgrund*], in which it fears to lose itself.[10]

Remarkably, Nietzsche uses the same word as Kant when in "The Dionysian Worldview" he goes about distinguishing between the beautiful and the sublime and aligning the Dionysian with the latter: "Dionysian man," says Nietzsche, "seeks to attain his *Vorbild* in the *Erschütterung* of sublimity" (III 2: 59).

The determination of tragedy that has been posed—not without the prospect of a suspending recoil—is: tragedy is a disclosing of the abyss as sublime. Now it needs to be asked: What is the structure of such tragic disclosure? How does the mimetic structure of tragedy serve to effect such disclosing? And what manner of turning is in play in the disclosure of the abyss *as* sublime? How is it that tragedy lets the abyss turn into the sublime?

10. Kant, *Kritik der Urteilskraft*, §27. I have discussed this passage in detail and in context in *Spacings—of Reason and Imagination. In Texts of Kant, Fichte, Hegel* (Chicago: University of Chicago Press, 1987), 126–27.

This determination of tragedy and the questions opened by it are addressed by a single, very remarkable sentence in *The Birth of Tragedy:*

Tragedy is seated in the midst of this excess [*inmitten dieses Überflusses*] of life, suffering and joy, in sublime ecstasy [*in erhabener Entzückung*], listening to a distant melancholy song that tells of the mothers of being whose names are: delusion, will, woe. (III 1: 128)

Here, if ever, there is need of that slow reading of which Nietzsche would be the teacher.

Several points connect the sentence directly to the determination of tragedy and the discourse gathered up in it. Tragedy is said to be in *sublime ecstasy:* it is that artistic ecstasy, that mimetic standing out into the abyss, that would disclose the Dionysian as sublime. Tragedy is said to be seated in the midst of this *excess of life:* this excess is the abyss into which one is thrown in exceeding the limits of the individuality characteristic of living beings, that is, the abyss is nothing other than the round of excess, the round of transgression, disruption, and reinstatement. Tragedy is said to be listening to a *song:* tragedy is born from music, from the Dionysian chorus, which imitates—though without images, thus without detachment—the abyss from which individuals will always have been reborn. And so, the song to which tragedy is said to be listening is one that tells of the *mothers of being;* another passage refers also to this phrase from *Faust,* identifying the mothers of being as "the innermost core of things" (III 1: 99). One of the notebook entries advises that "we should shun no abyss of thinking in order to discover tragedy near [*bei*] its mothers" (III 3: 97). The note concurs with the identification of the mothers as delusion (*Wahn*), will, and woe; and another note calls these three the names of the three abysses of tragedy (III 3: 370). Tragedy listens to a song that tells of delusion in which one is thrown beyond oneself into the round of what has been called will and has been conceived as being so at variance with itself as to spread suffering everywhere, universal woe.

Beyond thus resuming the determination of tragedy, the sentence on tragedy in sublime ecstasy provides two decisive indications that need to be deciphered in order to take up the questions opened by this determination. The first lies in the description of the song as a *distant* one. In this connection reference is made, not

to tragedy's singing the song (though in a sense it does, in the chorus, sing it), but rather to its *listening* to it *from a distance*. What,
then, is this distance that is installed in the tragic disclosure? How
does the mimetic structure serve to install it in the disclosing? The
second indication lies in the word that I have translated *excess*, the
excess in the midst of which tragedy is said to be seated. In contrast
to the more negative word *Übermass*, used throughout the discussion of the Dionysian and connoting *excessive*, Nietzsche now uses
the word *Überfluss*, which has also the positive aspect of superabundance, profusion. The engagement of life in both aspects is suggested by the appositional phrase following the word *life: suffering
and joy*. What, then, is the difference between *Übermass* and
Überfluss? How is it that tragedy discloses life as *Überfluss*, as suffering *and* joy?

The distance in the tragic disclosure points to the function of
the Apollinian mimesis within the total structure of tragedy; for
the Apollinian mimesis, the projection of the music into an image
(the dramatic scene), is precisely what produces the distancing.
Near the end of *The Birth of Tragedy* Nietzsche refers to this role
played by far-throwing Apollo:

Among the peculiar art effects of musical tragedy we had to emphasize an
Apollinian illusion [*Täuschung*] by means of which we would be saved
from immediate unity [*Einssein*] with Dionysian music, while our musical excitement could discharge itself [*sich . . . entladen*] in an Apollinian
field and in relation to a visible intermediary world that had been inter-
posed. (III 1: 145–46)

It should be noted here how Nietzsche retains a trace of Aristotelian catharsis, though indeed as a very subordinate moment
within the structure of tragedy. [11]
Let it be said, then, that within tragedy Apollinian mimesis
produces *distancing images*. Like all Apollinian images, those produced within tragedy have the character of shining. Hence,
Nietzsche refers to "the truly serious task of art," describing that
task in these words: "to save [*erlösen*] the eye from gazing into the
horrors of night and to deliver the subject by the healing balm of

11. The extent of this subordination, that is, Nietzsche's divergence from
the Aristotelian concept of tragedy, is indicated in the following notebook entry:
"*Against Aristotle*, who counted the ὄψις and the μέλος only among the ἡδύσματα
of tragedy: and already completely sanctioned the read-drama" (III 3: 78).

shining from the spasms of the agitations of the will" (III 1: 122). [12] Most notably, these images serve both to reveal and to conceal: they both set the Dionysian before one's eyes, make it visible, present as shining in the distance that which cannot as such be presented, be made present; and yet, thus projected into the distance, in the very radiance of their shining, the images limit that vision, draw one back from that gaze into the abyss that would be no vision at all of anything present. In the end, then, it is not even just a matter of both revealing and concealing, as though something were already present beforehand and simply in need of being illuminated, though perhaps not too brightly. Rather, the Apollinian mimesis operative in tragedy first opens the very space in which an il-luminating, a disclosive presenting, revealing and concealing, becomes possible—the very space of disclosure, the space of trag-edy. Even within this space, however, it is not a matter of presenting the Dionysian, of bringing it forth in a self-showing, for it remains as such unpresentable. What the Apollinian images present is, rather, the higher truth of the abyss thus imaged. The Apollinian mimesis within tragedy produces, at a distance, images of the *Dionysian in its higher truth*.

It is imperative to differentiate the effect of the Apollinian mi-mesis within tragedy, its letting images of the unpresentable Dionysian shine in the distance, from that pure objectification of the will that Schopenhauer regards as constituting ideas, which are, in turn, the objects of that pure perception, that contempla-tion, characteristic of art (WWV 1: §§34, 36). The differentiation is dictated by the fundamental difference between ideas in Schopenhauer's sense and Apollinian images as characterized by Nietzsche (see above, chap. 1 d). The differentiation is reflected also on the side of the spectator: for Nietzsche one does not, in the face of tragedy, become a disinterested, pure will-less subject, but rather one is shaken, made to tremble at the edge of the abyss. Thus, in contrast to Schopenhauer, tragedy is for Nietzsche no es-cape from willing and from the suffering implicated therein; it is no mere, temporary masking of the source of human misery but

12. In "The Dionysian Worldview" Nietzsche writes: "Apollo, the healing and atoning god, saved the Greeks from the clear-sighted ecstasy [*Ekstase*] and the disgust at existence—through the artwork of tragic-comic conception" (III 2: 60).

rather a disclosure capable of leading one back from pessimism to affirmation.

The higher truth that gets disclosed in tragedy is: the abyss as sublime. Nietzsche says that tragedy—in its Apollinian moment, one can add[13]—"places between the universal validity of its music and the receptive Dionysian listener a sublime parable, the myth." As a result that listener feels "as though the innermost abyss of things spoke to him perceptibly" (III 1: 130–31). That which cannot as such be presented comes to shine in the distance as sublime. It comes to be disclosed as that *Überfluss* of life in which suffering is conjoined necessarily with joy, in which "the struggle, the pain, the destruction of appearances, now seem necessary to us, in connection with [*bei*] the excess of countless forms of existence that force and push one another into life, in connection with the excessive fertility of the world-will" (III 1: 105). Like the Kantian sublime, the sublime abyss sets one tremoring, casts one into the movement of *Erschütterung,* overwhelming and exceeding one in such a way that one is drawn beyond narrow individuality to a universal destination. And yet, for Nietzsche that destination would be, not moral, but aesthetic: "for it is only as an *aesthetic phenomenon* that existence and the world are eternally justified" (III 1: 43)—or as Nietzsche writes when he almost repeats this statement near the end of the work: ". . . appear justified" (III 1: 148). It would be a matter not of subordinating the individual to the moral law, but of casting one into the dissonant play of the abyss:[14]

In this sense, it is precisely the tragic myth that has to convince us that even the ugly and disharmonic is an artistic play [*Spiel*] that the will in the eternal fullness of its joy plays with itself. But this primal phenomenon of Dionysian art is difficult to grasp, and there is only one direct way to make

13. Nietzsche expresses the relation into which the beautiful and the sublime enter in tragedy when he writes of the Apollinian: "it satisfies our sense of beauty which longs for great and sublime forms; it presents images of life to us and incites us to comprehend in thought the core of life they contain" (III 1: 133). The relation is expressed perhaps most succinctly when in "The Dionysian Worldview" Nietzsche says that with the advent of tragedy the Olympian gods "were dipped in the sea of the sublime" (III 2: 60). It is hardly necessary to remark that this relation between the beautiful and the sublime is something utterly different from the indifferent continuity that Schopenhauer would establish between them.

14. "In the end, Nietzsche conceives the oppositional *Walten* of Dionysus and Apollo as 'play' ['*Spiel*']" (Fink, *Nietzsches Philosophie,* 31).

it intelligible and grasp it immediately: through the wonderful significance of *musical dissonance*. Quite generally, only music, placed beside the
world, can give us a concept by which to understand what is meant by the
justification of the world as an aesthetic phenomenon. The joy aroused by
the tragic myth has the same origin [*Heimat*] as the joyous sensation of
dissonance in music. The Dionysian, with its primal joy experienced even
in pain, is the common womb of music and tragic myth. (III 1: 148)

In words that recall the transfiguring sufferings of blind Oedipus,
his clear descent into Hades, his wonderful end, Nietzsche writes
of the spectator:

He shudders at the sufferings that will befall the hero and yet anticipates
in them a higher, much more overpowering joy. He sees more extensively
and profoundly than ever and yet wishes he were blind. (III 1: 137)

For it is a matter of disclosing, in that which cannot as such be
presented, the play that connects suffering and joy, that prevents
either from cancelling the other, that holds them together in their
very opposition. As in seeing more deeply than ever yet wishing
one were blind. As in having to see at the very moment when one
also longs to transcend all seeing (III 1: 146). As with dissonance,
as in desiring to hear and at the same time longing to get beyond all
hearing (III 1: 149). As with that contradiction that is both more
and less than contradiction.

Tragedy both reveals and conceals the Dionysian abyss. And
yet, such revealing and concealing are no longer simply binary opposites, nor is the disclosure thus to be thought as a mere mean
between these opposites. In the determination of tragedy
Nietzsche is under way to a thinking of disclosure that would
differentiate it decisively from mere uncovering (limited by
a symmetrical opposite). For it is a matter of a disclosure of the
abyss, of that which withdraws from any presentation, of that
which cannot as such *be present* (or absent, as long as absence is
considered merely the complementary opposite of presence). It is
a matter of a disclosure in which, nonetheless, the unpresentable
is brought to shine in the distance as sublime. Thus, it is a matter
of a disclosure that first opens up the very space in which disclosure can come to pass. Tragic disclosure is a *spacing:* not only because it opens the very space of disclosure but also because within
that space the opposites are disclosed as spaced, as if a certain interval were inserted between them so as to allow them to persist

in their very opposition, both more and less than contradictory. In tragedy the "Dionysian phenomenon"—as Nietzsche finally calls it—becomes manifest in its dissonance, in its contradiction, in its power to hold in play, without synthesis, the oppositions between joy and suffering, reunion and dismemberment, construction and destruction:

Again and again it reveals to us the playful construction and destruction of the individual world as the overflow [Ausfluss] of a primal joy; in a way similar to that in which Heraclitus the Obscure compares the world-building force to a playing child who places stones here and there and builds sand hills only to overthrow them again. (III 1: 149)

d

Thus would Nietzsche read not only Heraclitus but indeed all the early Greek thinkers from Thales up to Socrates. All would be read in the direction bespoken by the title of the text on the Greek philosophers that Nietzsche wrote in the early 1870s but left unpublished: the early Greek thinkers belong to the *tragic age* of Greece, and access to their thought must take its bearings from their engagement with tragedy—with tragedy not as a particular form of art but as a unique spacing of disclosure. Such is the reading that Nietzsche undertakes in "Philosophy in the Tragic Age of the Greeks" and in the closely related lectures "The Preplatonic Philosophers," which he presented several times in the early 1870s in Basel. No doubt, his reading also places a certain emphasis on what he calls personality: "I want to emphasize only that point of each of their systems that is a slice of personality" (III 2: 295). No doubt, too, he leaves largely unthought the connection between this emphasis on personality and the orientation of his text to the tragic engagement of the early Greek thinkers. Perhaps, even, the emphasis on personality has the effect of obscuring the early Greek engagement with tragic disclosure. And yet, to conclude with Heidegger that Nietzsche establishes "a vital rapport with the personalities of the Preplatonic philosophers" while offering only "commonplace, if not entirely superficial" interpretations of the texts is to withdraw too quickly from the tragic element in which Nietzsche's reading would show the texts of the early Greek thinkers to be engaged. One can close Nietzsche's text in this manner, denying him the thoughtful experience of the history of Greek thought, only by passing over the engagement with tragedy as though it were in the end extrinsic to thought and not, instead, the very engagement that distinguishes the early Greek thinkers.[15]

In various ways and measures the Preplatonic thinkers are "tragic philosophers" (III 3: 122). When the philosopher first appears in Greece, he comes, says Nietzsche, with the same purpose as that for which tragedy was at the same time born (III 2: 302–3). One of the notebook entries is still more explicit: "The great thinkers of the tragic age reflect upon no other phenomenon than that which is taken up also by art" (III 3: 67). In tragedy and in the thought of the early Greek philosophers the phenomenon is the same: it is that phenomenon that, strictly speaking, is no phenomenon at all but rather the unpresentable abyss that tragedy lets shine in the distance as sublime. The space of tragedy is the space of such disclosure. Such, too, is the space of early Greek thinking, of its Dionysian engagement. Not unlike lyric poetry and tragedy, early Greek thinking is propelled by the power of phantasy: just as the phantasy of the poet or of the chorus sets forth image upon image, so the phantasy of the early philosophers leaps from possibility to possibility, illuminating similarities with lightning speed, drawing on toward that proposition that Nietzsche says is to be found in every philosophy, together with the ever renewed effort to express it more appropriately, the proposition: all is one (III 2: 307–8).

15. Heidegger also calls attention to Nietzsche's designation of these philosophers as Preplatonic and concludes: "The unexpressed standard for considering and judging the early thinkers is the philosophy of Plato and Aristotle." The same presupposition is said to be operative in Hegel, even though Heidegger reserves for him alone the distinction of having "thoughtfully experienced the history of thought": "Hegel too shares the predominant conviction concerning the classic character of Platonic and Aristotelian philosophy" and interprets the earlier thinkers specifically as "Prearistotelian" (Martin Heidegger, "Der Spruch des Anaximander," *Holzwege,* Gesamtausgabe 5 [Frankfurt am Main: Vittorio Klostermann, 1977], 323). Certainly one cannot forego such vigilance as that by which Heidegger would avoid submitting the early Greek thinkers to a standard drawn from later thinkers and put into effect in the very designations used for the earlier thinkers. And yet, for Nietzsche the designation *Preplatonic* does not at all signify that the earlier thinkers are to be measured by the standard of Platonic philosophy but, on the contrary, that their thought is quite incomparable to that which first appeared with Plato. Socratic-Platonic philosophy represents for Nietzsche a break, a rupture, a new beginning, rather than a standard to which everything preceding would be submitted.

From its beginning with Thales, philosophy is engaged with the Dionysian no less than is tragedy. And, as in tragedy, so too in philosophical thought it is a matter of setting out into another form, of translating, the music of the Dionysian. Nietzsche writes:

The philosopher seeks to let echo [*nachtönen zu lassen*] within himself the full sound [*Gesammtklang*] of the world and to set it forth in concepts. . . . What verse is for the poet, dialectical thinking is for the philosopher. (III 2: 311)

Thus, not only tragedy but also philosophy is born from music. One could say even—in the words of the original subtitle of *The Birth of Tragedy*—that both are born from the *spirit* (*Geist*) of music, though it would then be imperative to recognize that music, once it is determined in relation to the Dionysian, cannot be appropriated to the concept of spirit as determined in metaphysical thought. If music lets the unpresentable Dionysian resound, then it can never be assimilated to that self-presentation by which, with only rare exception, the concept of spirit has been determined: the spirit of music cannot be transformed into the music of spirit.

Both tragedy and philosophy translate music into another form, setting forth images or concepts. Regarded merely as translations, as means of communicating what has resounded within oneself, they are unfaithful, paltry means, stammerings in a foreign tongue (III 3: 311). For what they must translate is such as to withdraw from such translation: the resounding of ecstasy, of the movement of excess. And yet, when the Greeks, nonetheless, were compelled to stammer on in the alien languages of poetry and philosophy, what they produced—Greek tragedy and Preplatonic thought— provided the very archetypes of poetry and philosophy. Among the Greek philosophers appeared the original types, which later, beginning with Plato, came to be mixed and were rarely to be found again in their purity (W 19: 128–30; III 2: 304). The early Greek thinkers represent, says Nietzsche, the "incarnation of philosophy and of its various forms" (III 3: 409) as they come, in the original, upon the scene in the tragic age of Greece: Anaximander, Heraclitus, Parmenides, Pythagoras, Anaxagoras, Empedocles, and Democritus. [16] Nietzsche proposes to recover and recreate these

16. In his lectures Nietzsche is quite specific about these original types: "From Thales to the Sophists and Socrates we have seven independent rubrics, i.e., the appearance seven times of an independent, original philosopher: 1. Anaximander,

originals in order "to let the polyphony of the Greek nature finally sound once again" (III 2: 296).

In the fragment of Anaximander the lines of engagement with tragedy can be directly drawn. The fragment says, following Nietzsche's translation: "To that from which things arise they must also pass away, according to necessity; for they must pay penalty and be judged for their injustice according to the ordinance of time."[17] Nietzsche focuses on the link thus expressed between coming to be and passing away: all coming to be is construed as illegitimate emancipation, as an injustice for which destruction, passing away, is the penance that must be paid. It is as if Anaximander had thought cosmologically what Schopenhauer expressed on the plain of human existence: that human beings are creatures who ought really not exist at all and who must do penance for their existence by undergoing manifold suffering and finally death. In this case Anaximander could be said to have thought, on the plain of cosmology, the terrible wisdom of Silenus: what is best of all is—never to come to be; second best is—to pass away soon. What Anaximander thinks cosmologically and translates into utterance is the resounding of the Dionysian abyss. He attempts to think it as origin (*Ursprung*),[18] and yet as an abysmal origin it cannot be

---

2. Heraclitus, 3. Eleatics, 4. Pythagoras, 5. Anaxagoras, 6. Empedocles, 7. Atomists (Democritus)" (W 19: 157). Nietzsche goes on to qualify somewhat his inclusion of Pythagoras in this list: "He was not at all a philosopher, but something else. . . . He created the image of a kind of philosophical life: this the Greeks owe to him. This image exerts a powerful influence not on philosophy but on the philosophers (Parmenides, Empedocles)" (W 19: 158–59). On the other hand, later in the lectures he refers to Pythagoras, Heraclitus, and Socrates as "the purest types" (W 19: 172). One could perhaps also say—though Nietzsche does not do so explicitly—that Parmenides is the most extreme type: over against Heraclitus, whose engagement with tragedy is perhaps most direct and transparent, as the "counter-image" of Heraclitus, Parmenides would detach thinking, even if remaining in that very attempt determined by that with which he would break. With Parmenides there comes, in Nietzsche's words, "a moment of purest, quite bloodless abstraction, untroubled by any reality," a moment that was "un-Greek as no other in the two centuries of the tragic age" (III 2: 330).

17. Nietzsche's translation: "Woher die Dinge ihre Entstehung haben, dahin müssen sie auch zu Grunde gehen, nach der Notwendigkeit; denn sie müssen Busse zahlen und für ihre Ungerechtigkeiten gerichtet werden, gemäss der Ordnung der Zeit" (III 2: 312).

18. Nietzsche uses both *Ursprung* and *Princip der Dinge,* presumably translating ἀρχή and αἰτία, respectively. Neither word occurs in the extant fragment of

thought determinately; the "womb of all things" can only be thought as the indeterminate, as τὸ ἄπειϱον. Nietzsche says that it can only be designated "negatively" and compares it to the Kantian thing-in-itself, with which—curiously—it is said to be of equal birth (*ebenbürtig*) (III 2: 313). Thus engaged in thinking the Dionysian, Anaximander assumes the bearing of a tragic hero:

He lived as he wrote; he spoke as solemnly as he dressed; he lifted his hands and placed his feet as though this existence were a tragedy into which he had been born to play the hero. (III 2: 314–15)

Onto the scene came Heraclitus: "He raised the curtain on this greatest of dramas" (III 2: 329). His regal possession was his extraordinary power to think intuitively (*die höchste Kraft der intuitiven Vorstellung*), a power so extraordinary that it could prevail even against what Aristotle would later set forth as the law of contradiction. His sin lay in his "monstrous intuitions" (W 19: 173), in his intuiting a unity of opposites that exceeded in advance that oppositional exclusion that was later to be proclaimed the most unconditional of laws.

Nietzsche has him begin at the same site as Anaximander. But where Anaximander had seen only injustice, Heraclitus beholds the reign of justice. The Silenic vision of punishment for coming to be gives way to an intuition of the justification of becoming, an intuition of the rule of a certain order connecting perishing with becoming. Thus, from the beginning Heraclitus's thinking enacts a turn analogous to that which tragedy effects in withdrawing one from the abyss of Silenic wisdom. Through his intuitive thinking Heraclitus was brought also to efface the distinction between the indeterminate origin and the determinate world—that is, to think the Dionysian, not as a separated, indeterminate one (comparable to a Kantian thing-in-itself), but as the very movement of indetermination within the otherwise determinate world of the everyday. Disrupting the otherwise stable limits that would delimit things in their being, that movement of indetermination has the effect of

---

Anaximander, though they do occur in various versions of Theophrastus's account of Anaximander handed down by Simplicius, Hippolytus, and others. On the question whether Theophrastus attributes to Anaximander a use of the word ἀϱχή, see G. S. Kirk and J. E. Raven, *The Presocratic Philosophers* (Cambridge: Cambridge University Press, 1969), 107–8.

dissolving being into becoming. Heraclitus is led to proclaim: "I see nothing other than becoming":

For this one world that he retained—supported by eternal unwritten laws, flowing upward and downward in brazen rhythmic beat—nowhere shows a tarrying, an indestructibility, a bulwark in the stream. (III 2: 317)

And yet, such everlasting and exclusive becoming, such injection of indetermination into the very core of things, is "a fearful and paralyzing thought," virtually a return of the terrible wisdom of Silenus. The greatest power is required to transform this thought again—as tragedy does—"into the opposite, into the sublime and into blessed astonishment" (III 2: 319; cf. W 19: 179). Such a translation is what Heraclitus's monstrous intuition allows him to accomplish, namely, by thinking the unity of opposites in their opposition. Such unity in opposition he thinks under the form of polarity, as the divergence of a force into opposites, which seek to reunite but which also are forever reasserted in their opposition. Everything is thus seen to happen in and as this struggle: πόλεμος πάντων . . . πατήρ ἐστι (Fr. 53). Heraclitus exempts nothing from the struggle, not even the tribunal that otherwise would be set above in order to pass judgment and to proclaim from without the eternal justice of the struggle. The world is the play of the gods, and at least to the gods and to the philosopher this "sublime image" (III 2: 324) conveys that all contradiction flows also into harmony. In the shining of this image the all too limited, human vision of punishment and guilt gives way to a vision of the innocence of becoming:

In this world only the play of the artist and of the child displays a becoming and perishing, a building and destroying, without any moral attribution, in forever equal innocence. And as the child and the artist play, so plays the ever-living fire. It builds and destroys, in innocence—and this is the play that the aeon plays with itself. Transforming itself into water and earth, it builds towers of sand like a child at the seashore, builds them up and tramples them down. (III 2: 324)

In thinking *play*, Heraclitus thinks what tragedy lets shine forth on stage: the unity of joy and suffering, of reunion and dismemberment, of building and destroying, their unity in their very opposition. It is also what Nietzsche himself thinks in thinking the space of tragedy; and it is thus little wonder that in his very last turn back upon *The Birth of Tragedy*—in *Ecce Homo*—Nietzsche singles out Heraclitus as the one "in whose proximity I feel altogether warmer and better than anywhere else," as the teacher of "a Dionysian philosophy" that "is more closely akin to me than anything else thought to date" (VI 3: 310–11).

And yet, it is Empedocles whom Nietzsche calls the tragic philosopher: "He is the tragic philosopher, the contemporary of Aeschylus" (W 19: 194).[19] It is his extraordinary pessimism that Nietzsche finds most striking, a pessimism that issues, not in quietism, but in the very highest activity. It is a pessimism that Nietzsche links to Empedocles's view of earth as being only the scene of strife (νεῖκος) (W 19: 200). But it is also a pessimism overcome—as tragedy overcomes pessimism—insofar as Empedocles thinks also, together with strife, the opposed impulse, love (φιλία). Such is for Nietzsche "the properly Empedoclean thought," that of "the unity of everything that loves" (W 19: 196). Nietzsche notes that with Empedocles "mythical and scientific thinking go side by side"; as in Fragment 6, which Nietzsche cites in the lectures: "Hear first the four roots of all things: shining Zeus, life-bringing Hera, Aidoneus and Nestis who with her tears fills the springs of mortal men with water."[20] Such mixing is, says Nietzsche, "what makes him so difficult to understand." It is also what holds his thought in such proximity to tragedy and entitles him to be called the tragic philosopher.

In thinking the struggle (πόλεμος) between love and strife, Empedocles thinks the Dionysian movement of reunion and dismemberment. He thinks it cosmologically, that is, as the logos, the gathering, that determines the cosmos, that produces what Empedocles calls a double coming into being and a double passing away.[21] Nietzsche notes that the primary problem for Empedocles is that of the origination of the ordered world. The problem is:

19. "Music and tragedy, like the philosophy of Empedocles, signs of the same force" (III 3: 292).

20. Translation by Kirk and Raven, *The Presocratic Philosophers*, 323. Kirk and Raven concur with Nietzsche's conclusion that these four figures represent fire, air, earth, and water (W 19: 198); they note, however, that even in antiquity there was a difference of opinion regarding the exact correlation.

21. Fragment 17. See Kirk and Raven, *The Presocratic Philosophers*, 326.

How does such a world arise from the opposed impulses, without any imposition of a telos from outside (there is neither telos nor outside) and without the Anaxagorean hypothesis of a νοῦς guiding from within? Most remarkably, when Empedocles addresses the problem of this gathering that would come to pass solely in and as the struggle between the opposed impulses of love and strife, what he speaks of are *monsters:* the body of a bull (mis)attached to a human head, creatures at once male and female, and "all possible monsters" (W 19: 198). Love and strife—in their struggle—must play out the (re)gathering of parts into forms capable of life: "Here Empedocles is in agreement with Heraclitus's glorification of πόλεμος as the father of things" (W 19: 200). What he adds is a vision of the monstrosity that such begetting cannot but also produce.

Nietzsche's discussion of Empedocles in his lectures, though all too brief, suffices nonetheless to establish the lines of Empedocles's engagement with tragedy, showing how it is that Empedocles can be called the tragic philosopher or even, as one of the notebook entries puts it, "the pure tragic man" (III 3: 122). And yet, it is in other texts and in a quite different connection that Empedocles's proximity to tragedy is most powerfully attested. I refer to the plans and sketches of a tragic drama *Empedocles* which are found in the notebooks of 1870–71. David Krell has recently collected these plans and sketches and has discussed them in detail and with a view to the transformation that Nietzsche's proposed drama underwent.[22] Let it suffice here to cite only one sketch, which traces the course that Nietzsche's tragic hero would have followed. This sketch attests unmistakably to the affinity that the drama would have had to what Nietzsche thinks in *The Birth of Tragedy:*

Empedocles, driven through all the stages, religion, art, science, turns the latter against itself, dissolving it.
Departure from religion, through the insight that it is deception.
Now joy in artistic shining, driven from it through the recognized sufferings of the world. Woman as nature.
Now he observes the sufferings of the world like an anatomist, becomes *tyrannos,* uses religion and art, becomes steadily harder. He resolves to annihilate his people, because he has seen that they cannot be

22. David Farrell Krell, *Postponements: Woman, Sensuality, and Death in Nietzsche* (Bloomington: Indiana University Press, 1986), chap. 2.

healed. The people are gathered about the crater: he becomes mad and before he vanishes proclaims the truth of rebirth. A friend dies with him. (III 3: 130)

In these few lines so much of *The Birth of Tragedy* is invoked, even if with connections and turns that cannot but seem absolutely strange: the joy taken in that artistic shining that would veil the abyss of suffering, that abyss of which tragedy tells in its song of the mothers of being, a song of ecstasy, of madness, proclaiming the Dionysian truth of rebirth, making one tremble at the edge of the abyss; also the turning of science into self-dissolution, as if the Empedocles of the drama would leap to that point of rebirth that Western culture can reach only by traversing the long path from Socrates to Kant and Schopenhauer, and, beyond that, to the birth of another tragic philosopher.

Thus would Nietzsche have composed a dramatic double of the theoretically oriented discourse of *The Birth of Tragedy.* Had he composed it, such a dramatic double would, in turn, have reproduced, redoubled, from the side of tragedy the tension within which the entire discourse of *The Birth of Tragedy* is suspended, the opposition that cannot but divide that text from itself, making it an impossible book. That Nietzsche did not compose the drama can only strengthen the suspicion that this tension, this opposition between philosophy and tragedy, cannot be resolved in the unity of a single, homogeneous text.

In *The Birth of Tragedy* the other form of Greek drama remains marginal, except insofar as the so-called New Attic Comedy is said to further the dissolution brought on by Euripidean tragedy. And yet, in one key passage Nietzsche hints at a profound affinity between comedy and tragedy. The passage is one that is already familiar; I cite it now in full:

Here, when the danger to his will is greatest, *art* approaches as a saving sorceress, expert at healing. She alone knows how to turn these disgusting thoughts about the horror or absurdity of existence into representations with which one can live: these are the *sublime* as the artistic taming of the horrible and the *comic* as the artistic discharge of the disgust of the absurd. (III 1: 53)

Comedy would turn disgust with the absurd into the comic, as tragedy turns the horrible abyss into the sublime.[23] How might comedy do so? Perhaps in the way hinted at in a remarkable discussion of comedy found in Nietzsche's lectures, "History of Greek Literature" (1874–75). Nietzsche says of comedy:

It is a magnificent caricature, an inverted world, that the poet shows, sense and nonsense, reality and impossibility in crazy confusion. (W 18: 58)

Comedy, too, would be a supplement to nature, doubling it in such a way as also to overcome it. As in tragedy, the doubling would effect an overcoming by disclosing a certain unity of opposites in their opposition, a play of unity and duality. By means of caricature and inversion, comedy would open a certain vision of the play of crazy confusion, a play in which nonsense is shown to belong to sense and impossibility to reality.

23. In his "Attempt at a Self-Critique" (1886) Nietzsche hints at such a connection, referring to "that madness [*Wahnsinn*] out of which tragic as well as comic art developed, Dionysian madness" (III 1: 10).

SOCRATES —

Writing Music

a

Tragedy died tragically. It died as the result of an irreconcilable conflict, a conflict between tragedy as it had been attained and a new demand brought to bear upon it by Euripides. Thus it was he who fought the death struggle. [1] Tragedy died by suicide.

Where is the tragedy of tragedy written? Where is it to be read? Where is there a shrine commemorating the tragic death of tragedy? Where is there a monument on which this drama is inscribed?

Nietzsche identifies one such monument. After tragedy there appeared on the dramatic scene the New Attic Comedy of Menander and Philemon: therein "the degenerate form of tragedy lived on as a monument of its exceedingly painful and violent death" (III 1: 72). Tragedy comes to be enshrined in the New Attic Comedy; there its corpse lives on in the form of ever more degenerate imitations, enjoying posthumously its frivolous and eccentric old age, the senility of Greek cheerfulness. On this monument one can read of the death of tragedy, and indeed Nietzsche provides the outline of such a reading.

1. Without altering his view that Euripides is the decisive figure, Nietzsche sometimes suggests that the transformations that led from Aeschylean tragedy to the death of tragedy were already under way in Sophocles. In this regard he refers to "the prevalence of *character representation* and psychological refinement in tragedy from Sophocles on." He explains: "The character is no longer to be expanded into an eternal type but, on the contrary, is to develop individually through artistic subordinate traits and shadings, through the finest precision of all lines, in such a way that the spectator is in general no longer aware of the myth but of the vigorous truth to nature and of the artist's imitative power" (III 1: 109). In the 1870 lecture "Socrates and Tragedy" he is even more explicit that the decline began with Sophocles: "To speak quite openly, the flowering and the zenith of Greek music drama is Aeschylus in his first great period, before he was influenced by Sophocles: with Sophocles the quite gradual decline begins, until finally Euripides with his conscious reaction against Aeschylean tragedy brings about the end with impetuous haste" (III 2: 41).

The Bacchae, too, is a monument linked to the death of tragedy, granted Nietzsche's reading of Euripides's very late drama as a recantation of the poet's lifelong drive to exclude the Dionysian from tragedy. For by the time Euripides finally composed his palinode, ending his life "with a glorification of his adversary" (III 1: 78), Dionysus had already been driven from the scene of tragedy, leaving only its corpse. Beyond the death of tragedy, *The Bacchae,* scene of Euripides's suicide, opens the crypt and for a moment brings tragedy again to life. Here one can read perhaps the most direct and most powerful story of the life of tragedy; but not of the death of tragedy, not of its tragedy. Despite its link to the death of tragedy, *The Bacchae* is a monument, not of that death, but of a momentary rebirth of tragedy.

There are other shrines on which the tragedy of tragedy is inscribed, shrines in which is encrypted not merely the degenerate form of tragedy that resulted from the Euripidean death struggle, but that very struggle itself, the irreconcilable conflict between tragedy as it had been attained and the new demand brought to bear upon it. A paradigm of such a shrine is constituted by the discursive field bounded by two inscriptions, Aeschylus's *The Libation Bearers* and Euripides's *Electra.*[2] Across this field the tragedy of tragedy is written.

This inscription requires double reading. First of all, because it is linked to a double inscription: two dramas that enact the same story of Orestes's return from exile to carry out, with his sister Electra, his deadly revenge against his mother Clytemestra and the usurper Aegisthus. It is almost as if *Electra* were inscribed upon *The Libation Bearers,* written over it in such a way as to correct the faults that Euripides *as critic* found in the work of his predecessor. Hence another doubling in the reading: on the one hand, Euripides as critic, as spectator and judge of *The Libation Bearers;* on the other hand, Euripides as dramatist, writing *Electra.* And, conversely: tragedy as attained in *The Libation Bearers,* what Nietzsche would like to call tragedy itself, the essence of tragedy; and, on the other hand, the new demand brought to bear upon tragedy by Euripides. Yet, it is Nietzsche's text that exposes such doubling, such irrecon-

2. Translations are adapted from those by Richmond Lattimore (*The Libation Bearers*) and Emily Townsend Vermeule (*Electra*) in *Greek Tragedies,* ed. David Grene and Richmond Lattimore, vol. 2.

cilable conflict at the heart of the tragedy of tragedy; thus from the outset one will have deciphered these doublings only by a reading that, in turn, doubles them with Nietzsche's text. Only through such redoubling can one read the tragedy of tragedy.

The Libation Bearers begins at a shrine, at the tomb of Agamemnon.

The opening speeches serve "to place in the spectator's hands, as if by chance, all the threads necessary for understanding" (III 1: 82); yet slowly, one thread at a time, letting them interweave as if by chance.

Orestes speaks the first words, invoking the support first of Hermes and then of Zeus, asking that they grant him vengeance for his father's murder. Then comes a long choral song by the libation bearers accompanying Electra to the tomb: they sing of their grief, of a terror belled clear by a diviner of dreams, the terror of dead men under the earth smoldering still at their murderers. The chorus sings of the godless woman to whom the dream has come (not yet naming her), the woman who has sent them forth bearing libations; also of a man (unnamed, almost uncharacterized) who goes in fear. They sing of the futility of bearing the libations:

What can wash off the blood once spilled upon the ground?
(LB 48)

And again:

Through too much glut of blood drunk by our fostering ground
The vengeful gore is caked and hard, will not drain through.
The deep-run ruin carries away
The man of guilt. Swarming infection boils within.
(LB 67–70)

Only much later does the chorus reveal to Orestes the content of Clytemestra's dream: her dream was that she gave birth to a snake, that giving it her breast to suck, the beast tore at her nipple and drew in blood along with the milk. Orestes himself then interprets the dream:

I
Turn snake to kill her. This is what the dream portends.
(LB 549–50)

And still later Clytemestra herself—to Orestes:

> You are the snake I gave birth to and gave the breast.
>
> (LB 928)

But in the opening the chorus unfolds the story slowly, lyrically, as if by chance. It is from the chorus, the libation bearers (χοηφόροι), that the drama is named in its Aeschylean inscription. Only after the great choral song does Electra, from whom the other inscription will be named, come to speak. She is among the libation bearers, a projection of the chorus onto the scene of the drama, a projection spanning the very space of tragedy.

Electra weaves another thread into the tangle by betraying that her mother is implicated in the murder. Yet she does not yet voice the indictment directly but rather expresses it by referring to her own entanglement:

> What shall I say, as I pour out these outpourings
> Of sorrow? How say the good word, how make my prayer
> To my father? Shall I say I bring it to the man
> Beloved, from a loving wife, and mean my mother? I
> Have not the daring to say this, nor know what else
> To say, as I pour this liquid on my father's tomb.
>
> (LB 87–92)

Thus it is as libation bearer that Electra first speaks. Only after the ensuing, extended exchange with the chorus does she finally draw together the entire story that precedes the opening of the drama. Her prayer for the return of Orestes sets the stage then for the recognition scene.

Nietzsche has no doubt but that Euripides viewed this opening scene quite differently: as critic he thought he observed that during the initial speeches "the spectator was so anxious to solve the problem of the prehistory that the poetic beauties and the pathos of the exposition were lost for him." Thus as critic what he notices in the opening scene are missing links, gaps in the prehistory, which cannot but interfere—so he reasons—with the hearer's "pleasurable absorption in such scenes" (III 1: 84). Especially in such choral songs as that at the beginning of *The Libation Bearers:*

He observed something incommensurable in every feature and in every line, a certain deceptive determinateness [*Bestimmtheit*] and at the same time an enigmatic depth, indeed an infinity of background. Even the clearest figure always has a comet's tail attached to it which seemed to suggest the uncertain, the unilluminable. (III 1: 76–77)

Thus Euripides the critic, the thinker, submitted tragedy as it had been attained to a demand for illumination, for intelligibility, the demand that what is to be beautiful must be intelligible.[3] Faced with *The Libation Bearers* he could only confess that he did not understand his great predecessor; or, rather, he could not but insist that the story be reinscribed so as to be clearly understandable. When he reinscribes it as *Electra,* he has it begin with a prologue: "So he put the prologue even before the exposition and placed it in the mouth of a person who could be trusted" (III 1: 82). The prologue with which *Electra* begins is put in the mouth of a poor farmer who is so trustworthy that he has lived with highborn Electra without ever touching her, her husband in name only. Now the prehistory is told openly and in the proper order, beginning with Agamemnon's departure for Troy and ending with Aegisthus's disposing of Electra by giving her to the farmer. Having related the story, the farmer then tells who he is, presenting his treatment of Electra as testimony to his trustworthiness and hence to the truthfulness of the story he has recounted.

By this device and others Euripides brought "the man of everyday life" (III 1: 72) onto the stage. He withdrew tragedy from the abyss, back toward the everyday.[4] He "brought the spectator onto the stage"; under the demand for intelligibility he brought forth on the stage "the faithful [*treue*] mask of reality" (III 1: 72). Images of the everyday now came to be shown on stage, displacing those images capable, in their shining, of making manifest the Dionysian. Reproductions of the everyday came to replace "the grand and bold traits" displayed by the Dionysian heroes of the older trag-

3. Thus in the 1870 lecture "Socrates and Tragedy" Nietzsche characterizes Euripides as the first dramatist whose creative work is governed by an explicit aesthetic: "Euripides is the first dramatist who consciously follows an aesthetic. He deliberately seeks what is most intelligible [*das Verständlichste*]: his heroes really are just as they speak. But they also express themselves completely, while the Aeschylean-Sophoclean characters are much deeper and fuller than their words: they really only stammer about themselves. Euripides creates his figures by dismantling them at the same time: because of his anatomy there remains nothing concealed in them" (III 2: 31).

4. With Euripides "the figures of everydayness [*Alltäglichkeit*] came clearly into prominence" (III 2: 26).

edies. In *Electra* Orestes has little, if any, of his former heroic stature, clubbing Aegisthus to death while the latter, having hospitably invited Orestes to join in the sacrifice, is bent over the sacrificial flesh of the bull (cf. E 839–41). And, in the words of one interpreter, "Electra, sorry for herself and making an exhibition of her mistreatment, seems an all too lifelike parody of her tragic predecessors."[5] Removed from the tomb and from the entanglement of libation bearing, removed to a timber-and-mudbrick cottage in the countryside, Electra is now made to utter such humble proverbs as:

> When a man comes in from work
> It is sweet to find his hearthplace looking swept and clean.
>
> (E 75–76)

Or such commonplaces as:

> O what perversion, when the woman in the house
> Stands out as master, not the man.
>
> (E 932–33)

The removal of the scene from the tomb to the country also serves to make *Electra* more truthful to reality, more plausible: the success of Orestes's murderous revenge is much more understandable if carried out in a remote country spot rather than in the palace. Yet the way in which *Electra* is written over *The Libation Bearers* under the direction of a critic who would correct the original inscription is nowhere more obtrusive than in the recognition scene. In *The Libation Bearers* a lock of hair left by Orestes at the tomb reveals his presence to Electra by proving to match exactly with her own hair. Another sign confirms that presence: footprints that likewise match exactly those of Electra. In *Electra* Euripides corrects the scene, substituting the more plausible process in which the old man who had once saved young Orestes from death recognizes him by a scar above his eye. But Euripides is not content merely to correct the scene; he also unmistakably mocks the form that the recognition scene took in the Aeschylean inscription: when the old man, having discovered a lock of hair at the tomb, suspects that it may announce the return of Orestes and asks Electra to match it with her own hair, she quickly challenges his

5. Richmond Lattimore, Introduction to *Electra* in *Greek Tragedies*, 2:182.

assumption that the hair of the brother must match exactly that of the sister:

> Besides, how could a lock of his hair match with mine?
> One from a man with rugged training in the ring
> And games, one combed and girlish? It is not possible.
> You may find many matching birds of the same feather
> Not bred in the same nest, old man, nor matched in blood.
>
> (E 527–31)

Likewise with the old man's plea that she go and set her foot in the print made by the boot of the one who has visited the tomb:

> How could rocky ground receive
> The imprint of a foot? And if it could be traced,
> It would not be the same for brother and for sister,
> A man's foot and a girl's—of course his would be bigger.
>
> (E 534–37)

Set on correcting the scene, venturing even to mock it, Euripides would no doubt have listened with the most critical ears to the following exclamation by Electra in *The Libation Bearers:*

> The bitter wash has surged upon my heart as well.
> I am struck through, as by the cross-stab of a sword,
> And from my eyes the thirsty and unguarded drops
> Burst in a storm of tears like winter rain, as I
> Look on this strand of hair.
>
> (LB 183–87)

No doubt his judgment of such language would have been, as Nietzsche puts it: "too much pomp for simple affairs, too many tropes and monstrosities for the simplicity of the characters" (III 1: 77).

Euripides could not but have seen something monstrous also in the way the ethical problems were resolved by his predecessor: "And how dubious the solution of the ethical problems remained to him" (III 1: 77). The problem of Orestes's guilt is paradigmatic. In *The Libation Bearers* Orestes reports that the Delphic Oracle has charged him to revenge the murder of his father, warning him that otherwise he must pay penalty with his own life (LB 269–77). The choral response lyricizes and reinforces Orestes's proclamation of his mission:

> Almighty Destinies, by the will
> Of Zeus let these things
> Be done, in the turning of Justice.
> . . . .
> The spirit of Right
> Cries out aloud and extracts atonement
> Due: blood stroke for stroke of blood
> Shall be paid. Who acts, shall endure. So speaks
> The voice of the age-old wisdom.

(LB 306–8, 310–14)

After the murders are accomplished, Orestes again appeals to the Oracle, saying:

> He
> Declared I could do this and not be charged with wrong.

(LB 1030–31)

Again the choral response is affirmative:

> No, what you did was well done. . . .
> . . . .
> You liberated all the Argive city when
> You lopped the heads of these two snakes with one clean stroke.

(LB 1044–47)

And yet, the furies approach, and Orestes must flee,

> . . . an outcast wanderer from this land.

(LB 1042)

Little wonder that Euripides rewrote almost entirely the closing scene of the drama,[6] closing off the drama by means of the Dioscuri's proclamations concerning the murder of Clytemestra:

> Justice has claimed her but you have not worked in justice.
> As for Phoebus, Phoebus—yet he is my lord,
> Silence. He knows the truth but his oracles were lies.

(E 1244–46)

6. In this regard the closing scene of Sophocles's *Electra* would likely have appeared to Euripides as equally in need of reinscription. For the final words of Sophocles's Orestes are:
> Justice shall be taken
> Directly on all who act above the law—
> Justice by killing. So we would have less villains.

Furthermore, in the Sophoclean inscription there are no Furies and no flight of Orestes (Sophocles, *Electra,* tr. David Grene, in *Greek Tragedies,* vol. 2).

But the silence is soon broken:

> On Phoebus I place all
> Guilt for this death.
>
> (E 1296–97)

Thus the *deus ex machina* comes to close the drama, assuring the audience of the future just as the trustworthy farmer had in the prologue given assurance about the past. In the end everything is rounded out: what is beautiful is to be intelligible.

The demand for intelligibility comes to determine Euripidean drama as a whole. The coolness of thought with which Euripides designs it[7] is also set into the drama itself, informing the speech of the characters:

The spectator now essentially saw and heard his double on the Euripidean stage and rejoiced that he could speak so well. But this joy was not all: one could even learn from Euripides how to speak oneself. Upon this he prides himself in his contest with Aeschylus: how from him the people have now learned to observe, debate, and draw conclusions according to the rules of art and with the cleverest sophistries. (III 1: 73)

One need only compare the final exchange between Orestes and Clytemestra in *The Libation Bearers* with the dialogue that Euripides inscribes at the same dramatic moment between Electra and Clytemestra. Electra's discourse is most remarkable, and no doubt the people could have learned from it how to observe, debate, and draw conclusions. It poses argument and counterargument (Clytemestra's argument that she killed her husband because he had sacrificed their daughter Iphigenia is only a screen to hide her treachery and unfaithfulness), marshals evidence for the counterargument (long before the sacrifice of Iphigenia, as soon as Agamemnon set out, she was setting her brown curls, working on her beauty in a way that in the absence of her husband indicted her as a whore), extends the counterargument (even if Agamemnon killed Iphigenia, still Electra and Orestes did Clytemestra no harm worthy of the treatment they have received), and ends by rigorously drawing its conclusion:

7. A notebook entry from 1869: "Euripidean tragedy is, just like French tragedy, formed according to an abstract concept" (III 3: 35).

119

> If murder judges and calls for murder, I will kill
> You—and your own Orestes will kill you—for father.
> If the first death was just, the second too is just.

(E 1094–96)

The coolness of thought that Euripides brought to the drama is complemented by the fiery affects displayed by his characters. Thus Orestes after the murder of his mother:

> You saw her agony, how she threw aside her dress,
> How she was showing her breast there in the midst of death?
> My god, how she bent to earth
> The legs which I was born through? and her hair—I touched it—

(E 1206–9)

He continues:

> She cracked into a scream then, she stretched up her hand
> Toward my face: "My son! Oh, be pitiful my son!"
> She clung to my face,
> Suspended, hanging; my arm dropped with the sword—

(E 1214–17)

Corresponding differences are to be found in Euripides's handling of the chorus. To the enigmatic and lyrical speech of the chorus in the opening scene of *The Libation Bearers,* one could hardly imagine a greater contrast than that provided by the first choral speech in *Electra:* the chorus speaks only after the drama is well under way, and the speech merely passes along word heard on the road about a feast at which a procession of maidens is to mount to the temple of Hera. When the chorus speaks again what they say has the sound of friendly advice: do not lament, but love the gods, and gentler days will come for you (E 166–74, 190–98). To say nothing of the contrast between the final speeches of the choruses. Aeschylus:

>   Where
> Is the end? Where shall the fury of fate
> Be stilled to sleep, be done with?

(LB 1074–76)

Euripides:

> Farewell. The mortal who can fare well,
> Not broken by trouble met on the road,
> Leads a most blessed life.

(E 1037–39)

Nietzsche says that Euripides "transferred the entire world of sentiments, passions, and experiences, hitherto present at every festival performance as the invisible chorus on the spectators' benches, into the souls of his stage-heroes" (III 1: 76). Thus, the stage-heroes come to dominate,[8] while the chorus, the musical womb of tragedy, is displaced into a role, becoming little more than another character: the libation bearers are replaced by Electra and some peasant women. The choral character could almost be put on stage with the others, and then the space of tragedy would have been utterly reduced. It is precisely this reduction that is played out in the Euripidean death struggle.

Thus did Euripides attempt—in the very midst of this struggle—to reconstitute tragedy, to reinscribe *The Libation Bearers* outside the Dionysian element. Apollo, too, he finally drove out with that fiery passion that precluded all epic absorption in images shining from a distance. Hence, Euripides sought to base tragedy on elements lying outside "the only two art-impulses, the Apollinian and the Dionysian": "cool, paradoxical *thoughts*—replacing Apollinian contemplation—and fiery *affects*—replacing Dionysian ecstasies [*Entzückungen*]" (III 1: 80).

Euripides finally recanted, even though by then his tendency had so triumphed that not even *The Bacchae* could arrest it. Indeed, Euripides had been all along, says Nietzsche, only a mask through whom another spoke, one neither Apollinian nor Dionysian, the newborn daimon called Socrates. Behind the death struggle of Euripidean tragedy there is a new opposition, and this new opposition is what produces that irreconcilable conflict from which results the tragic death of tragedy: "This is the new opposition: the Dionysian and the Socratic—and the art of Greek tragedy was wrecked on this" (III 1: 79).

8. In the 1870 lecture "The Greek Music Drama" Nietzsche writes of this shift: "Just a single step further and the scene dominated over the orchestra, the colony over the mother-city; the dialectic of the stage-characters and their individual songs came into prominence and overpowered the hitherto operative choral-musical, total impression. This step was taken, and Aristotle, contemporary with it, established it in his famous, very confusing definition, which does not at all fit the essence of Aeschylean drama" (III 2: 15).

b

Socrates—"this most questionable phenomenon of antiquity" (III 1: 86).

First of all, because of what he called into question and condemned. Plato has him tell the Athenian court how throughout the city he found only the conceit of knowledge: responding audaciously to the utterance of the Delphic Oracle, calling that utterance into question in such a way as to shelter his assurance of his own ignorance, he set about questioning those reputed to know, only to discover that they lacked insight even into the very arts they practiced, relying more on instinct than on knowledge. Assured of his ignorance and through the Oracle declared superior precisely in that assurance, Socrates could regard such reliance on instinct only as serving to conceal and compensate for the ignorance of those whom he questioned, concealing it even from themselves. Even if some of them were eminently successful in governing the city, even if others composed beautiful works of art or even sublime tragedies, even if the artisans among them could produce the most splendid artifacts, concealed ignorance lay behind their doing and making; and that ignorance could not but determine what was done and made by instinct, infusing even sublime tragedy with an incommensurability, with an enigmatic depth that gives the appearance of being unilluminable. Thus Socrates could not but join Euripides in confessing that he did not understand tragedy; or, rather, secure in his assurance of ignorance, he could not but suspect that what lies behind all its incommensurable features and lines is only concealed ignorance and that its depth is enigmatic only because, as long as such ignorance remains concealed, it limits the drive to illuminate the depths. Little wonder that Socrates did not esteem tragedy, that he condemned it: wherever he looks, testing and questioning what he finds before him—Nietzsche refers to *seine prüfenden Blicke*—"he sees lack of insight and the power of illusion [*Macht des Wahns*] and from this lack infers the intrinsic perversity and reprehensibility of what is present" (III 1: 85)—that is, condemns it.

Socrates is thus the most questionable phenomenon of antiquity also because of what he opposed and succeeded in destroying. Nietzsche would have him bear the responsibility, first of all, for the destruction of tragedy: speaking through Euripides, casting *seine prüfenden Blicke* from behind that mask, it is as if he guided the hand of Euripides in the reinscription that proved to be tragedy's death struggle. Nietzsche refers to the story current in Athens that Socrates used to help Euripides write his plays, even though, in a now famous note from 1869, Nietzsche describes Socrates as the nonwriter (*der Nichtschreiber*) (III 3: 13). Did he, even in guiding the hand of Euripides, remain the nonwriter, following instead *seine prüfenden Blicke,* even opening perhaps the most secure differentiation between writing and vision? Did he remain the nonwriter even in helping to write tragedy?

It is too soon to link this question to that of the Apollinian and to take up the question of Socrates's relation to the Apollinian. That his is a mission provoked by the Delphic Oracle serves to indicate that the relation is anything but simple. Yet however that question may stand, there can be no question but that Nietzsche sets him in opposition to Apollinian art and regards him as having provided the basis for destroying it: the theoretical genius, of whom Socrates is the paradigm, is the "destroyer of Hellenic Apollinian art" (III 3: 139). Indeed, such was the strength of the Socratic mission that he opposed not only the entirety of Greek art from Homer to Sophocles but also the science and philosophy of his great predecessors. The *Phaedo* tells of his turn away from such science, from περὶ φύσεως ἱστορία. It tells also of the δεύτερος πλοῦς—which Nietzsche would assign to Socrates, struggling to differentiate him from Plato[9]—that is, the second voyage on which Socrates's turn is to λόγοι, a turn, therefore, from vision to that which, already inscribed in language, can be set forth as ὑπόθεσις, almost a turn to writing. At the same time, Socrates brought thinking back from the heavens into the city, brought it into service to life. In the lectures "The Preplatonic Philosophers," Nietzsche calls Socrates the first philosopher of life (*Lebensphilosoph*) and his philosophy an absolutely practical philosophy: "Thinking serves life, whereas with all earlier philosophers life served thinking and knowing" (W 19: 227). Thinking serves what previously

9. In his lectures "Introduction to the Study of the Platonic Dialogues" (1871–76), Nietzsche discusses the Platonic account of the δεύτερος πλοῦς, struggling to differentiate between Socrates and Plato by means of references to Xenophon and Aristotle. He concludes: "Thus this genesis does not correspond to Plato's. . . . Rather it refers to Socrates, yet without our being able to say to what extent Plato has presented the probable development of Socrates and to what extent a history that he actually knew. In any case it is not his own" (W 19: 285–86).

had been served by instinct, by the ethical instinct; Nietzsche says that "Heraclitus, Anaxagoras, Democritus, Empedocles breathed Hellenic ethicality [*Sittlichkeit*]" (W 19: 228). And though Nietzsche leaves it unsaid, Socrates could not but have heard behind the concepts of the earlier thinkers the echo of that same cosmic music that he denounced in tragedy as a mask of ignorance.

Socrates is thus the most questionable phenomenon of antiquity also because of what he inaugurated: the service of thought to life, the demand for intelligibility, even at the cost of being obliged to guide the hand of the artist. And yet, he cannot have lent his vision and even his hand without the risk of contamination by the artist. He cannot but have risked becoming an artistic Socrates. It is as such a figure that Socrates, this most questionable phenomenon of antiquity, is a sign of hope for the present and the future.

Socrates—"a true monstrosity *per defectum.*"

The monstrous divergence is betrayed by the phenomenon of Socrates's daimon. For it is not a matter only of an absence of instinctive wisdom in Socrates. Even for him there are moments, even if rare ones, when a voice of instinctive wisdom intervenes, the voice of his daimon. What is decisive is that the daimon always dissuades, so that the natural relation between instinct and conscious knowledge is inverted:

> In this utterly abnormal nature instinctive wisdom appears only in order to *hinder* conscious knowledge occasionally. While in all productive men instinct is the creative-affirmative face and consciousness acts critically and dissuasively, in Socrates instinct becomes the critic and consciousness becomes the creator—a true monstrosity *per defectum*. (III 1: 86)

What is monstrous is the lack of the natural relation between instinct and conscious knowledge, that is, the divergence from nature lies in the inversion. In the phenomenon of the daimon it is manifest that the Socratic world is so inverted as to be perverted, *eine verkehrte Welt*, a true monstrosity. [10]

Nietzsche adds that Socrates has "a monstrous *defectus* of any mystical disposition" (III 1: 86; cf. III 3: 235). On the other hand, his logical nature is said to be excessive, as excessively developed as

---

10. The figure of *die verkehrte Welt* appears in the 1870 lecture "Socrates and Tragedy": "Here too it becomes manifest that Socrates really belongs to an inverted world, to a world stood on its head [*einer verkehrten und auf den Kopf gestellten Welt*]" (III 2: 34).

instinctive wisdom is in the mystic. What is this so-called logical nature and how is it opposed to the mystic and the instinctive? Is it to be defined by reference to the turn to λόγοι? Nietzsche does not say. In any case, what is it that drives the Socratic logical nature to such monstrous excess? What is the impelling force of that logical Socratism that Nietzsche is now prepared to differentiate from Socrates himself, the Socratism behind Socrates, the Socratism that "must be viewed through Socrates as through a shadow" (III 1: 87). [11] Nietzsche does not identify this monstrous driving-wheel (*das ungeheure Triebrad*) but says only that its power is such as is encountered only in "the very greatest instinctive forces." One may well suppose that it is only because it possesses such power that Socratism is capable of displacing instinct from the creative center to the critical margin. But it is imperative to forego leaping to the conclusion that what is behind the Socratic displacement of instinct is just another instinct, thus reducing Socratism to a mere action of instinct upon instinct. Its structure is more complex, more differentiated, if for no other reason than that it involves the reflective assurance of ignorance.

Nietzsche marks another monstrous defect displayed by Socrates: his lack of natural awe, of fright (*Schauder*), in the face of death. Such a lack is displayed by Socrates in the depiction of his trial: Nietzsche suggests that Socrates deliberately brought it about that he was sentenced to death, "with full awareness and without any natural awe of death" (III 1: 87). In *The Birth of Tragedy* Nietzsche does not mention that the Socrates of the *Phaedo* is portrayed as an exorcist charming away the natural fear of death, doing so precisely by discoursing on death with his friends, that is, by way of philosophy. But elsewhere, at that point in his lectures on Plato where he discusses the *Phaedo,* Nietzsche does mention both the exorcizing of the fear of death and the posing of death as "the genuine, inspiring genius of philosophy," which is thus determined as the practice of dying (θανάτου μελέτη). A monstrous

11. Referring to a certain perplexity about the chorus manifest in Sophocles and the beginning therefore of a breakdown of the Dionysian basis of tragedy, Nietzsche speaks of "an anti-Dionysian tendency operating even prior to Socrates" (III 1: 91). In the lecture "Socrates and Tragedy" he is explicit about a Socratism prior to Socrates: "Socratism is older than Socrates; its art-dissolving influence can be noticed much earlier. Its characteristic element of dialectic crept into the music drama a long time before Socrates" (III 2: 37).

determination and one that Nietzsche, struggling to differentiate them, would assign to Plato, not to Socrates (W 19: 258; cf. 301).

Socrates is another kind of monster: "Let us imagine the one great Cyclops eye of Socrates fixed on tragedy, an eye in which the gentle madness of artistic enthusiasm has never glowed." A single eye sees no depth, or, rather, tends to see depth only as additional surface: it is "denied the pleasure of gazing into the Dionysian abysses" (III 1: 88). With his Cyclops eye Socrates has, in Fink's words, no eye for the dark, night-side of life, [12] for the enigmatic depth that extends beneath the figures of tragedy. To the Cyclops eye of Socrates, tragedy cannot but appear quite irrational (*etwas recht Unvernünftiges*), marred by gaps and missing links not only in the opening and closing scenes—as Euripides thought—but throughout.

Socrates—the nonwriter.

Or, now, to write it as Nietzsche does: the "nonwriter." Thus he marks the difficulties that cannot but accumulate around this designation, the slippage that sets in, for instance, as soon as one supposes that Socrates guided the hand of Euripides, as soon as one accords the slightest weight to the report that Socrates helped him write his dramas.

Nietzsche writes: "Socrates as the 'nonwriter': he wants to communicate nothing, but only to question [*erfragen*]" (III 3: 13). And yet, he cannot *only* question, for questioning must turn back toward itself; and when it does so it produces a narrative of its own mission, origin, and orientation, like those that Socrates is depicted as presenting to the Athenian court and to those friends with him in prison on the day of his death. The question of the question is not just another question, and one would need to rewrite it within quotation marks so as to indicate the slippage, for instance, toward narratives of mission, origin, and orientation. Such narratives communicate something and bring Socrates closer to writing.

They are of course written, inscribed in that art form, the dialogue, that Plato created and bequeathed to posterity as

---

12. "Socratism no longer has an eye for the 'life' flowing behind all figures, constructing and destroying them" (Fink, *Nietzsches Philosophie,* 19). "With Socrates . . . man loses, as it were, his openness to the dark, night-side of life" (ibid., 28).

(Nietzsche suggests) the model of the novel. The writing is very different even from that of Euripides: "Here *philosophical thought* overgrows art and compels it to cling close to the trunk of dialectic" (III 1: 90). Indeed, one might well suppose that a certain remote affinity with the Apollinian cannot but remain in the Platonic text by virtue of the turn it inscribes from the everyday toward a sphere in which the everyday would be perfected (the sphere of the εἴδη that shine in and through the things of everyday vision); and yet, Nietzsche insists that Socrates—to whom he attributes the δεύτερος πλοῦς (W 19: 285–86)—is something entirely newborn, neither Apollinian nor Dionysian. Nietzsche is convinced that not even Plato's rich artistic endowment could lure the god back once he had been driven away by the hand of Socrates. Despite Plato's "great dramatic gifts" (W 19: 238), all that would remain of Apollo in the new artistic-philosophical form would be "the shell of logical schematism" (III 1: 90). [13]

And yet, Nietzsche can virtually exclude Apollo from the Platonic dialogues only by passing all too quickly over the shining of the εἴδη. In his lectures on Plato, Nietzsche touches on the question of such shining, specifically in the context of a debate with Schopenhauer concerning the origination of Plato's so-called theory of ideas. Nietzsche argues that this "theory"—I write it with quotation marks to indicate that it cannot be simply a theory, since it is the opening that determines the very sense of θεωρία, to indicate thus the reinscription of Nietzsche's text that would be required—originated from reflection not on the so-called sensible world but rather on moral concepts:

It would be possible for someone to arrive at the supposition of the ideas by consideration of the *visible* world: but Plato did not arrive at the supposition in this way. . . . The theory of ideas does *not* have its genesis in consideration of the visible world. Thus it does not have an aesthetic origin: for aesthetic contemplation presupposes the possibility of intuition [*dass angeschaut werden kann*]. However, Plato did not arrive at the theory of ideas on the basis of the intuitable, but only on the basis of such *nonintuitive concepts* as justice, beauty, equality, good. (W 19: 274)

13. In "Socrates and Tragedy" Nietzsche writes: "In Socrates *one* side of the Hellenic, that Apollinian clarity, was embodied without any heterogeneous additions" (III 2: 36).

This refusal to allow the "sensible" a role in the Platonic turn to the εἴδη should be read together with Nietzsche's attribution of a "hatred of sensibility" to both Socrates and Plato (W 19: 267). In any case, the utterly conventional and reductive character of Nietzsche's interpretation of Plato is evident in his unquestioning reliance on the opposition between intuition (*Anschauung*) and concept (*Begriff*), as if that opposition were not itself determined (and at a rather derivative level) by the Platonic opening, as if it had fallen from heaven and could be brought to bear directly on anything and everything, no questions asked. The character of Nietzsche's interpretation, especially in the lectures, stands out perhaps most remarkably if contrasted with the reference that *The Birth of Tragedy* makes to the *Symposium,* at the end of which Socrates's companions "remain behind to dream of Socrates, the true eroticist" (III 1: 87). Yet, even in this context it is as though Nietzsche simply drops the image he has so dramatically posed, or, rather, replaces it with another, that of the dying Socrates.

Nietzsche tends also to regard the Socratic-Platonic position regarding art as determined by opposition to shining. For instance, in a note from 1869–70 he writes:

Plato's hostility to art is something very significant. The tendency of his teaching, the way to truth through knowledge, has no greater enemy than beautiful shining [*schönen Schein*]. (III 3: 74)

It is as if Plato had not written the *Phaedrus* with its Socratic celebration of that most exceptional εἶδος, the beautiful, as the most shining (τὸ ἐκφανέστατον). [14]

But if Apollo, "the 'shining one' [*der 'Scheinende'*]" (III 1: 23), cannot be made to remain so alien to the Platonic dialogues—and indeed the most decisive passage is yet to come—then what of the Dionysian? Can one be assured that the unmistakably mythical substratum of the *Republic* is one to which Dionysus is utterly alien—even if the name around which that mythical underground is assembled is Hades? Can Plato simply have forgotten the Her-

14. One of the notebook entries points, however, to a residual relation between Socratism or science and shining: "All science directed to shining [*Schein*], insofar as it is firmly attached to individuation and never acknowledges the essential unity. In this sense it is Apollinian" (III 3: 166). Hence the sense of another note: "Socrates—the Apollinian individual, who . . . comes forth against Dionysus" (III 3: 165).

aclitean identification of Hades with Dionysus? Can one be assured that the good crossing to which Socrates gestures at the end of the *Republic* is so utterly alien to the rebirth that tragedy would celebrate?

Similar questions can be asked with regard to Socrates himself, especially considering how open to question it is whether there is a Socrates himself that can be rigorously differentiated from the Socrates that is depicted in the texts of Plato, Aristophanes, and Xenophon, to say nothing of the modern depictions by Hegel, Kierkegaard, and Nietzsche himself. Sarah Kofman has recently reopened with new precision the question of such differentiation and has attempted to demonstrate the impossibility of an interpretation of Socrates that would not be a "reappropriative fiction."[15]

In this context Kofman refers to an enigmatic note in which Nietzsche refers to Socrates as follows: "He is at the same time Prometheus and Oedipus, but Prometheus before his theft of fire and Oedipus before he solved the riddle of the sphinx" (III 3: 238). Kofman observes: "He is brought together with the great figures of Greek tragedy, Oedipus and Prometheus, who under an Apollinian appearance let a Dionysian monstrosity be divined."[16] Mentioning the comparison that Nietzsche draws between the driving force of Socratism and the greatest instinctive forces, she goes on to refer to "an excess, monstrous because it is Dionysian," by which "the wisdom of Socrates communicates with the great figures of Greek tragedy, with Prometheus, with Oedipus." The figure of Socrates, she concludes, involves a *dionysisme caché*.[17] Here one must be vigilant, on guard against reducing, flattening out, the opposition between Socrates and the Dionysian. For Nietzsche never fails to insist on the opposition, not only in *The Birth of Tragedy* but in note after note; for example, most directly: "Socrates, the opponent [*Gegner*] of Dionysus" (III 3: 169). If, nonetheless, one is to attribute a *dionysisme caché* to Socrates, it must be in order to render the opposition less symmetrical, less subject to simple dialectical reversal. Also, one must be attentive to the mutation that is announced by the qualification *caché*, to the transformation that the

15. Sarah Kofman, *Socrate(s)* (Paris: Galilée, 1989), 21.
16. Ibid., 19.
17. Ibid., 303–4.

Dionysian cannot but undergo in being concealed and in being concealed in the specifically Socratic mode. Socrates can be identified only with a Prometheus and an Oedipus in whom the Dionysian excess has not yet burst forth so as to become manifest, a Prometheus before the theft of fire, an Oedipus who has not yet solved the riddle of the Sphinx.

Socrates the nonwriter one has always sought to differentiate from, most notably, Plato the writer and from the Socrates written by Plato. It is this possibility that Kofman challenges:

And above all, in the dialogues of Plato how is one to choose between the diverse images of Socrates? How is one to make the division between what belongs to Socrates and what belongs to Plato? How is one to succeed in separating this inseparable pair and in capturing a "pure and authentic" Socrates, uncontaminated by his disciple, untransfigured by that one who, as the result of a slightly excessive and suspect filial piety, attributes to Socrates *all* his thought, never speaks in his own name, practicing more than anyone the mimetic discourse condemned in Books 2, 3, and 10 of the *Republic?* [18]

The Platonic dialogues, Kofman would suggest, are precisely such that they tend to render the difference between writer and nonwriter undecidable: what is written belongs in every case to a voice other than the writer's, a voice which, in the case of Socrates the nonwriter, is nonetheless always written.

Jacques Derrida approaches the same question, referring to Nietzsche in that regard as *un peu naïf sur les bords:*

Like everyone else he believed that Socrates did not write, that he came before Plato who more or less wrote at his dictation and therefore let him write by himself, as he says somewhere. From this point of view, N. believed Plato and overturned nothing at all. The entire "overturning" remained included in the program of this credulity. [19]

Derrida's strategy—reading and rereading that post card that on first reading appears to depict Plato dictating to a Socrates who is writing—is to reach the point where "one begins no longer to understand what to come [*venir*], to come before, to come after, to

18. Ibid., 17.

19. Jacques Derrida, *La Carte postale. De Socrate à Freud et au-delà* (Paris: Flammarion, 1980), 25. English translation by Alan Bass, *The Post Card. From Socrates to Freud and Beyond* (Chicago: University of Chicago Press, 1987), 20.

foresee [*prévenir*], to come back [*revenir*] all mean—along with the difference of the generations, and then to inherit, to write one's will, to dictate, to speak, to take dictation, etc."[20]

Socrates—the "nonwriter." And yet, Plato writes of one occasion when, it seems, Socrates did write. This occasion, this profound experience, is such that it prompts Nietzsche to begin a shift away from the symmetrical opposition of Socratic to artistic that the discourse on the death of tragedy served to establish. It is such as to impel him to ask "whether there is *necessarily* only an antipodal relation between Socratism and art or whether the birth of an 'artistic Socrates' is something altogether contradictory [*etwas in sich Widerspruchsvolles*]" (III 1: 92).

The occasion is the one about which Plato has Socrates tell his friends in prison. Often he has had a dream, the same dream, one in which he is told to practice music. Up to his final days he has assumed that his philosophizing was the highest art of the muses and that the reference was not to common music. But finally, in prison he decides to unburden his conscience by practicing music in the common sense. Thus he writes a prelude to Apollo and sets some Aesopian fables to verse.

Socrates—writing music.

Or, rather, Plato writing about Socrates writing music. About his writing music at the behest of Apollo. About his writing music in honor of Apollo. The story opens an Apollinian crack in the machinery of Socratism, in its driving-wheel, throwing that wheel ever so slightly off balance: perhaps art is not simply the opposite of Socratic science. Perhaps the opposition is not such as to submit only to a logic of noncontradiction or at best to a dialectical logic. In Nietzsche's words: "Perhaps art is even a necessary correlate and supplement of science" (III 1: 92).

What if Socratism, thus both opposing and supplementing art, were such as not only to direct the death of Greek art but also to prompt a rebirth of art? Then one could indeed see in Socrates the decisive turning point, the vortex into whose whirl all of history would be drawn. The name of Socrates, this most questionable phenomenon of antiquity, would serve not only to mark the ancient turn from tragedy to science but also to portend the turn that *The Birth of Tragedy* comes finally to announce, the turn that is al-

20. Ibid., 26 (E.T. 121).

ready addressed when Nietzsche writes of a "vortex and turning point" in the "Foreword to Richard Wagner" (III 1: 20).

Socrates—"the one turning point and vortex of so-called world history" (III 1: 96).

C

Now a different tone is sounded: "Here we knock, deeply moved [*bewegten Gemüthes*], at the gates of present and future: will this 'turning' ['*Umschlagen*'] lead to ever new configurations of genius and especially of the music-practicing Socrates?" (III 1: 98). The question is preeminently one of a single new configuration that *The Birth of Tragedy* would announce: a question of a turn at which Socratism comes to its limit and is overturned, awakening the spirit of music and opening the way to the appearance of a music-practicing Socrates, to a rebirth of tragedy.

Socratism, the stance of the theoretical man, is a certain engagement in uncovering. Nietzsche draws the contrast with the artist:

In every uncovering of truth the artist will always cling with rapt gaze to what still remains covering [*Hülle*] even after such uncovering; but the theoretical man enjoys and finds satisfaction in the discarded covering and finds the highest object of his pleasure in the process of an ever happy uncovering that succeeds through his own efforts. (III 1: 94)

Socratism is engagement in *unlimited uncovering;* Socratic man, theoretical man, lives under the demand for unlimited uncovering. Yet, this demand can be effective and the engagement sustained— with such power as is encountered only in the greatest instinctive forces—only by virtue of a certain representation (*Vorstellung*). At least that is how Nietzsche designates it in a note written in 1870 that is otherwise virtually identical with the passage just cited: the representation of removing all the covering (III 3: 141), the representation that things can be stripped down to their naked truth. By the time of *The Birth of Tragedy,* Nietzsche calls this *Vorstellung* a *Wahnvorstellung,* an illusion, a profound illusion "that first came into the world in the person of Socrates: the unshakable [*unerschütterliche*] belief that thought, guided by causality, can extend into the deepest abysses of being and that thought is capable not only of knowing being but even of correcting it" (III 1: 95). Nietzsche calls it a sublime illusion, as if to call attention to the contrast that the word *unerschütterliche* marks with tragedy, with the *Erschüt-*

terung that sublime tragedy produces; but also as if to indicate that, like sublime tragedy, Socratism saves one from the pessimistic wisdom of Silenus. The illusion has to do with the abyss, with reaching into it, as it were, both "theoretically" and "productively," both in thought and in deed; it has to do with illuminating the abyss, with dissolving the enigmatic depth that tragedy would only make manifest as such, and it has to do with correcting what is abysmally amiss, with eliminating the indetermination that otherwise can always surprise and threaten the individual. [21]

Nietzsche says that the illusion accompanies science as an instinct (*als Instinct*). And yet, it cannot do so as one instinct alongside others, as one instinct with which Socratism allies itself against others, for Socratism would drive all instincts to the margin of consciousness. If something instinctive remains in the power of the illusion that drives Socratism, it can only be an *instinct caché*. For Socratism, on the other hand, the power driving one on to unlimited uncovering would be inseparable from that of the assurance of ignorance.

One could say, then, that Socratism is not just the demand for—and satisfaction in—unlimited uncovering, but also the operation that lets the demand be effective and that sustains Socratic man's engagement in uncovering. That operation involves an illusion; it is an operation of closure, an operation that closes off the abysmal, Dionysian element so powerfully that total uncovering, naked truth, comes to be constituted as the ideal of Socratism.

All of this one *could* say, but *only* from a certain limit, a certain point where the illusion would have ceased to operate, where enigmatic depth would have become manifest in its unfathomability. What Nietzsche writes cannot have been written from within Socratism but only from a limit at which Socratism will have been overturned. Nietzsche cannot merely have written of the turn but also must have written *from out of the turn*. His writing must itself already have entered into the turn toward the music-practicing Socrates. Little wonder that it sounds a different tone.

Nietzsche says that science, led by its empowering illusion,

21. Here again one sees how Socratism is allied with the Apollinian by virtue of its advocacy of individuation. And yet, that advocacy, unfolding as unlimited uncovering, displays a lack of limit that sets it at odds with the Apollinian. An extract from a notebook entry makes the point: "Theoretical man, . . . Unlimited Apollinianism, boundless search for knowledge" (III 3: 140).

comes again and again to its limit at which it turns into art, at which it is overturned into its supplement, which thus emerges as supplement and not merely as opposite. In Nietzsche's words: "But science, spurred by its powerful illusion, speeds incessantly toward its limits where its optimism concealed in the essence of logic runs aground." It is a matter of reaching those limit-points on the periphery at which Socratic man comes to "gaze into the unilluminable." Nietzsche continues: "When he sees here to his horror how logic coils up at these limits and finally bites its own tail— suddenly the new form of insight breaks through, *tragic insight* which, merely to be endured, needs art as a protection and remedy" (III 1: 97).[22]

Thus Nietzsche broaches what one could call a kind of quasi-teleology operative in Socratism. I call it *quasi*-teleology for two reasons. First, because Nietzsche's text is not entirely uniform in presenting it as a single process that runs its course from Socrates to nineteenth-century German philosophy, the course that today one would call (almost) the (entire) history of metaphysics: in *The Birth of Tragedy* one finds also indications of repetition, statements that Socratism "again and again [*immer wieder*] prompts a recreation of art" (III 1: 93; cf. 95). Secondly, I want to indicate that the teleology is not one imposed from without but rather one constituted in the very dynamics of Socratism. It is a matter of Socratism's running a certain course, following a certain trajectory, at the end of which its limits come to be exposed, indeed exposed by Socratism itself as it doubles back upon itself, uncovering finally, at the limit, the very operation of closure, of concealment, that empowered it from the beginning.[23] Thus it is that at this limit a certain tragic

22. In a notebook entry entitled "Art and Science" (written between winter 1870–71 and spring 1872) Nietzsche begins by referring to the artistic-mystical *defectus* of Socrates and then, further in the note, writes: "Logic as an artistic tendency [*Anlage*], it bites its own tail and lets the world of myth open up. The mechanism by which science turns into art—1. at the limits of knowledge, 2. from out of logic." The note concludes by referring to "tragic man as the music-practicing Socrates" (III 3: 234).

23. Nietzsche also mentions, though briefly, a corresponding limit at the socio-political level: the optimism of Socratism, with its belief that it can correct what is most profoundly amiss, gives rise to the belief in—and then the demand for—the earthly happiness of all. The turn, Nietzsche says, comes through the conflict between the need to maintain a slave class and the optimistic view of life that denies the necessity of such a class. Hence, the Alexandrian culture based on

insight breaks through, namely, the gaze into the Dionysian abyss reopened at this limit. Exposed again to the threat of Silenic wisdom, one rediscovers the profound need of art.

At the limit, exposing it as limit, science is employed against itself, employed in such a way as to reveal its own limits. Nietzsche proposes that such a limit is constituted in the thought of Kant and Schopenhauer, in which is demonstrated the impossibility of knowledge of the essence of things, of the thing-in-itself.[24] Here the very instruments of Socratism are used to show that Socratic uncovering will never succeed in reaching the naked thing itself, that there will always remain a profound depth behind it, something unilluminable.[25]

Thus it is in the texts of Kant and Schopenhauer that the limit of Socratism comes to be inscribed. Nietzsche constantly enforces that inscription, reinscribes the limit more rigorously, even at the cost of a certain turn against Schopenhauer's tendency to extend knowledge surreptitiously toward the noumenal abyss by means of simple opposition to appearances. Yet, on the other hand, it is Schopenhauer who, even beyond Kant, opens the way from the sceptism of the self-destruction of Socratism to the gaze beyond the limit into the abyss.[26]

Socratism "gradually drifts toward a dreadful destruction. There is nothing more terrible," Nietzsche continues, "than a class of barbaric slaves who have learned to regard their existence as an injustice, and now prepare to avenge, not only themselves, but all generations" (III 1: 113). In this regard Nietzsche considers the loss of myth decisive and links this loss to Socratism and to the historicizing tendency of modern culture (III 1: 142).

24. The role of Kant is elaborated in a passage in *Schopenhauer as Educator:* "Kant has had a living and life-transforming influence on only a very few men. . . . If Kant ever should begin to exercise any wide influence we shall be aware of it in the form of a gnawing and disintegrating scepticism and relativism; and only in the most active and noble spirits who have never been able to exist in a state of doubt would there appear instead that undermining and despair of all truth such as Heinrich von Kleist for example experienced as the effect of the Kantian philosophy" (III 1: 351).

25. In "Socrates and Tragedy" Nietzsche writes: "For the infinitely more profound Germanic consciousness, Socratism appears as an altogether inverted world [*verkehrte Welt*]" (III 2: 33).

26. An excerpt from *Schopenhauer as Educator* makes the point: ". . . if we are to understand what, after Kant, Schopenhauer can be to us—namely, the leader who leads us from the heights of sceptical gloom or criticizing renunciation up to the heights of tragic contemplation . . ." (III 1: 352).

And yet, what *The Birth of Tragedy* would announce is not only the end of Socratism and the renewed exposure to the abyss (i.e., Schopenhauerian pessimism), but finally the *rebirth of tragedy.* Over against the Socratic destruction of tragedy:

What hopes must revive in us when the most certain auspices guarantee *the reverse process, the gradual awakening of the Dionysian spirit* in our modern world! . . . Out of the Dionysian ground of the German spirit a power has arisen which, having nothing in common with the primal conditions of Socratic culture, can neither be explained nor excused by it, but which is rather felt by this culture as something terribly inexplicable and over-whelmingly hostile—*German music,* as we must understand it, particularly, in its vast solar orbit from Bach to Beethoven, from Beethoven to Wagner. (III 1: 123).

After the self-destruction of Socratism and the renewed exposure to the Dionysian abyss, tragedy is to be reborn from German music. What *The Birth of Tragedy* would finally announce is "the Wagnerian rebirth of tragedy."[27]

What is, then, the relation between Socratism and the tragedy that is (or is to be) reborn? What is to be understood by the figure of the music-practicing Socrates? Is it a matter of regression from Socrates to the tragedy born of the practice of music? Is it a matter of becoming again Presocratic? There are passages that suggest this; for example: "we live through, as it were, the chief epochs of the Hellenic nature analogically in *reverse* order and seem now, for instance, to be passing backward from the Alexandrian age to the period of tragedy" (III 1: 124).[28] And yet, Nietzsche continues: "At the same time we have the feeling that the birth of a tragic age simply means a return to itself of the German spirit"—that is, the rebirth of tragedy would not produce a mere repetition of what was created by the Greeks. In this regard one of the notebook entries should be cited:

The goal of science, which Socrates inaugurates, is tragic insight as prepa-

27. "From the Greeks we can learn what we ourselves experience. They interpret our experiences for us. Sophocles was visited by Asclepius. Thus have we to understand the Wagnerian rebirth of tragedy. From being Socratic men we are to become again tragic men" (III 3: 392).

28. A note from 1870–71 reads: "Germany as backward-stepping Greece: we have reached the period of the Persian wars" (III 3: 101).

ration for genius. The new stage of art was not attained by the Greeks: it is the Germanic mission. (III 3: 214)[29]

It is presumably to such a new stage of art, an art of genius, that one should refer Nietzsche's remark in *The Birth of Tragedy* that the genius of music is "not to be judged by the standard of eternal beauty any more than by that of the sublime" (III 1: 123). Tragedy reborn would surpass even the sublime tragedy of the ancients.[30]

Even if Nietzsche would retain a certain regressive moment— assuming that his text is not in this regard simply heterogeneous—it would appear that the figure of the music-practicing Socrates signifies the transition to an art that would not as such simply be opposed to the Socratic. What perhaps best suggests such a relation is the slippage, the nonsymmetrical character, of the opposition by which the Socratic-Platonic is opposed to the Apollinian and to the Dionysian. How, then, would tragedy and (self-overcoming) Socratism now belong together? How are they united in the music-practicing Socrates? Can it be only a matter of synthesis, such that in the rebirth of tragedy Socratism would, in its very self-overcoming, be submitted to an *Aufhebung?* Or is the nonsymmetry of their relation not such as to resist reduction to synthesis? How, then, do they belong together? How is the simple mimetic structure of Socratism (that of uncovering, of theoretical truth) to be—precisely at its limit—thought together with the complex Apollinian-Dionysian structure of tragic mimesis?

29. This note could be read with a passage in a letter to Gersdorff written a little more than a year earlier. Nietzsche mentions the two public lectures on Greek tragedy that he is to present in Basel early in 1870 ("The Greek Music Drama" and "Socrates and Tragedy") and says that "Wagner will come from Tribschen to attend them." He continues, referring to Wagner: "I have already written telling you how invaluable this genius is to me, as the flesh-and-blood illustration of what Schopenhauer calls a 'genius' " (BKG II 1: 61).

30. The following notebook entry suggests some of the directions in which the question of the music-practicing Socrates could move: "In view of that mysterious and recurrent command by the dream apparition, 'Socrates, practice music,' we cannot avoid the question whether we may at all conceive of a music-practicing, i.e., artistically productive, Socrates: in connection with which it could in turn prove doubtful whether we would have to represent such a Socrates as being of the same type as Euripides or as Plato; unless thereby a thoroughly unique type is meant, who, in a new blending [*Verschmelzung*] of Apollinian and Dionysian, would also inaugurate an entirely new world. The latter is what we surmise [*unsere Muthmassung*]" (III 3: 235).

d

Nietzsche did not pursue these questions, at least not in what he wrote during the time of *The Birth of Tragedy*. Indeed, it is only at the margin of his text that these "theoretical" questions can be gathered, even beyond the limit where Socratism—which determines the sense of *theoretical*—disrupts itself, thus withdrawing that determination, requiring the quotation marks of another writing.

Nietzsche's writing in *The Birth of Tragedy* also undergoes a certain shift, though a different one. In the later sections of Nietzsche's book there are of course many passages that reiterate and reformulate the analyses and results developed in somewhat more rigorous order up through section 15; in fact, several of the most decisive formulations come only in the later sections. Nevertheless, toward the end of the book Nietzsche's discourse tends to shift away from the theoretical and away from its limit, sliding toward the music-practicing of the music-practicing Socrates, toward writing music (after the end of the book, inasmuch as the *sens* of [the] book is determined by Socratism).

Even before the shift there are passages that point to a renewed writing of music, as in Beethoven, and a rebirth of tragedy. As regards the latter, special note should be taken of Nietzsche's references to Shakespeare. As early as section 7, Nietzsche draws a comparison between the Dionysian man and Hamlet: the point is that Hamlet is one who has been exposed to the Dionysian abyss and who, having seen how abysmally the world is out of joint, is inhibited from acting (III 1: 52–53). It is a matter of exposure to Silenic wisdom and of projection of the Dionysian echo upon the stage, where, as Nietzsche observes, Hamlet "speaks more superficially than he acts" (III 1: 106). The tendency of the interpretation could hardly be clearer: *Hamlet* read as a tragedy crossing Apollinian and Dionysian in just the manner analyzed in *The Birth of Tragedy*.

Still more remarkable are the comments about Shakespeare found scattered in Nietzsche's notebooks of this period. Following Wagner, he associates Shakespeare with German music.[31] For ex-

31. For instance, Wagner writes in *Beethoven:* "Shakespeare therefore remained entirely beyond comparison [*unvergleichlich*] until in Beethoven the German genius brought forth a being only to be explained through his analogy. If we take the

ample, in a note from 1870–71, he mentions the beginning launched by Socrates and Euripides and then refers to the task of the future, as if it would also carry on the Socratic-Euripidean posture so as to produce a form for which Greek tragedy would only have been preparatory. Regarding this task Nietzsche then writes: "Heretofore only Shakespeare and our music are fully adequate [*entspricht*] to it" (III 3: 211). Another note from the same period, referring to the decisive influence of the Romans on subsequent art, remarks that "only the primal German spirit [*der urgermanische Geist*] in Shakespeare, Bach, etc., has emancipated itself from them" (III 3: 339). Perhaps most remarkable is the series of notes in which Shakespeare is described as bringing Greek tragedy, specifically Sophocles, to fulfillment. One such note goes so far as to identify him as the music-practicing Socrates: "Shakespeare the poet of fulfillment, he brings Sophocles to completion, he is the music-practicing Socrates" (III 3: 201).[32] Another, calling him again the completion of Sophocles, continues: "Completely Dionysian. He points to the limits of Greek tragedy: the same relation as between the old Greek music and German music" (III 3: 334).

Nonetheless, it is the rebirth of tragedy from German music that *The Birth of Tragedy* primarily announces, the Wagnerian rebirth of tragedy. Nietzsche even suggests that it is for the sake of understanding the Wagnerian music dramas that he turns to Greek tragedy. For example, in a note written in early 1871: "*What does tragedy mean for us?* From the Greeks we are to understand the Wagnerian artwork" (III 3: 393). And in a letter to a publisher to whom he sent a partial draft of *The Birth of Tragedy* in 1871, he writes: "The real task, however, it to throw light on Richard Wagner, the extraordinary enigma of our age, in his relation to Greek tragedy" (BKG II 1: 194).

---

total impression made by Shakespeare's world of shapes upon our innermost feeling, with the extraordinary precision of every character that moves therein, and hold it up to the whole of Beethoven's world of motives [*Motivenwelt*], with their ineluctable incisiveness and definition, we must see that the one of these worlds completely covers the other, so that each is contained in each, no matter how different may seem the spheres in which they move" (RW 9: 88).

32. Two related notes: (1) "The birth of *thought from music* appears in Sophocles only in a shadowy manner in *contemplation of the world*. Completion in Shakespeare: authentically German: to give birth to thought from music" (III 3: 332); (2) "In Shakespeare *thought* has become adequate to music" (III 3: 326).

By 1870 Nietzsche had become a regular visitor at the Wagner home in Tribschen. Wagner was completing *The Ring of the Nibelungen* and also in that year published a book entitled *Beethoven*. Nietzsche read the book with an enthusiasm born no doubt of his friendship with Wagner and reflected in his references to the work in several letters written toward the end of 1870. To Rohde he described the work as containing "a philosophy in Schopenhauer's spirit and with Wagner's force" (BKG II 1: 159); shortly thereafter he wrote again to Rohde, with whom he was discussing plans to found a "monastic-artistic community," "a new form of academy": "A recent book of Wagner's on Beethoven will give you a good idea of what I desire of the future. Read it—it is a revelation of the spirit in which *we*—we!—shall live in the future" (BKG II 1: 166). About the same time Nietzsche sent a copy of the book to Gersdorff and wrote to him: "I am sending you Wagner's latest work, on Beethoven. . . . I read it in a mood of elation and reverence. There are deep secrets in it, beautiful and terrible, as are the profoundest revelations of music itself" (BKG II 1: 161). Nietzsche refers explicitly to Wagner's *Beethoven* in *The Birth of Tragedy*, mentioning in the "Foreword to Richard Wagner" that it was precisely during the period when *Beethoven* appeared that he collected himself for the reflections that led to his own book. The coincidence is reflected in the text of *The Birth of Tragedy*, in the discussion advocating Wagner's position that music is not to be judged by the category of beauty; in this discussion Wagner's work is explicitly mentioned.

From the outset of *Beethoven*, Wagner emphasizes precisely the difference that prescribes withdrawing music from the rule of the category of beauty. Recalling Schiller's observation that the epic leans toward the plastic arts whereas drama is inclined toward music, he notes that it was, in fact, Schopenhauer who first defined the position of music in such a way as to show that it is of a totally different nature from the plastic arts (RW 9: 43). It is this difference that Wagner undertakes to think through in the first part of his work. Following Schopenhauer, he characterizes tone as a direct utterance of the will; on the other hand, Wagner reorients somewhat the characterization of the plastic arts, broaching a certain divergence from Schopenhauer, by stressing in particular the involvement of the plastic arts with shining (*Schein*); he even proposes a connection between *Schein* and *Schönheit* (RW 9: 48). Wagner's intent is to oppose the extension of the corresponding aesthetics of beauty beyond the plastic arts, that is, to protect and elaborate the difference between the arts of *Schein,* on the one hand, and music (along with drama), on the other. His conclusion is that "music can be judged only according to the category of the *sublime,* since, as soon as it engrosses us, it excites the highest ecstasy of consciousness of our boundlessness [*die höchste Ekstase des Bewusstseins der Schrankenlosigkeit erregt*]" (RW 9: 56). Here, too, Wagner not only extends but also diverges from Schopenhauer, moving unmistakably in the direction that Nietzsche resumes in *The Birth of Tragedy,* even in the direction of those passages and those notes from the same period that prompt a reinscription of Nietzsche's text outside the metaphysics of the will. In any case, it is clear even from the surface of Wagner's text how thoroughly he prepared here the monstrous difference that Nietzsche is to think as that between Apollinian and Dionysian. There is also much in Wagner's work that broaches the crossing of Apollinian and Dionysian in tragic drama: perhaps most notably, his characterization of drama "as the visible counterpart of music [*als sichtbar gewordenes Gegenbild der Musik*]" (RW 9: 94) and his observation that in Greek tragedy "the drama was projected from out of the choral song onto the stage" (RW 9: 104). Thus Wagner outlines the space of tragedy.

Little wonder, then, that Nietzsche could dedicate *The Birth of Tragedy* to Wagner and that the "Foreword to Richard Wagner" could, like a reinscribed preface, inscribe the book within a certain circuit of exchange with Wagner. Little wonder, too, that in drafting a letter on the day he sent his newly published work to Wagner, he could write to Wagner—even if with some exaggeration—that everything he has to say about the birth of Greek tragedy "has been said more beautifully, clearly, and convincingly by you" (BKG II 1: 270–71).

Indeed, it is striking that when Nietzsche comes finally to write directly about Wagner, in *Richard Wagner in Bayreuth* (1876), there are so many echoes of *The Birth of Tragedy.* For example, Nietzsche's discussion of the relation of art to nature leads to the following characterization of German music: "this music is a return to nature, while being at the same time the purification and the transformation of nature" (IV 1: 28)—an echo of an art that is "a metaphysical supplement of the reality of nature, placed beside it for its overcoming" (III 1: 147). Another passage introduces *cross-*

ing (*Kreuzung*), the crossing in the soul of the Dithyrambic dramatist, producing a crossing which, though Nietzsche stops short of calling it such, unmistakably echoes that of Apollinian and Dionysian: "What has hitherto been invisible and inward escapes into the sphere of the visible and becomes appearance; what was hitherto only visible flees into the dark ocean of the audible" (IV 1: 43). Still another passage refers to the primal nature expressed in music, describing it as "the most enigmatic thing under the sun, an abyss [*Abgrund*] in which force and goodness are coupled [*gepaart*], a bridge between the self and the nonself" (IV 1: 37); one cannot but hear an echo of discourse on the abysmal character of the Dionysian, on its self-disrupting movement of transgression, and also an echo of the discourse on the coupling of opposites. In this last regard, another passage recalls, perhaps most remarkably, the original bond between philosophy and tragedy: "Wagner's music as a whole is an image of the world as it was understood by the great Ephesian philosopher: a harmony produced by conflict, the unity of justice and enmity" (IV 1: 66).[33] Such a coincidence between Wagner and Heraclitus cannot but prompt the question of a certain coincidence between Wagner and Nietzsche, as their writings prove to be ever more thoroughly woven together. Will they ever have been utterly disentangled?

In *The Birth of Tragedy* itself there are only a few explicit references to Wagner: the Foreword, of course; a passing reference in section 7; the reference (in section 16) to the inappropriateness of the category of beauty for judging music; and, finally and most significantly, the announcement (in section 19) of the rebirth of tragedy from German music "in its vast solar orbit from Bach to Beethoven, from Beethoven to Wagner" (III 1: 123). And yet, following this announcement Nietzsche's discourse begins to slide in the direction of a certain repetition of, a certain coincidence with, Wagner's music dramas.

One passage refers to *Lohengrin:* Nietzsche refers to the effect that the music drama might have on a person nobly endowed by

33. With this passage should be read one in *The Birth of Tragedy* where Nietzsche writes of German music: "for in the midst of all our culture, it is really the only genuine, pure, and purifying fire-spirit [*Feuergeist*] from which and toward which, as in the teaching of the great Heraclitus of Ephesus, all things move in a double orbit: all that we now call culture, education, civilization, must some day appear before the unerring judge Dionysus" (III 1: 124).

nature but reduced to cultural barbarism by contemporary society; Nietzsche observes that such a person "might have something to say about the unexpected as well as totally unintelligible effect that a successful performance of *Lohengrin,* for example, had on him— except that perhaps there was no helpful interpreting hand to guide him" (III 1: 140). Thus Nietzsche hints at the gesture that *The Birth of Tragedy* would offer.

Another passage refers to *Tristan and Isolde.* It begins with the question whether one can conceive of "a man who would be able to perceive the third act of *Tristan and Isolde* without any aid of word and image, purely as a monstrous symphonic movement, without expiring in a spasmodic unharnessing of all the wings of the soul" (III 1: 131). To the state of one "who has thus, as it were, put his ear to the heart chamber of the world will," Nietzsche contrasts what happens when the tragic hero appears, enacting the myth on stage. With his appearance the force of the Apollinian restores the almost shattered individual:

Suddenly we believe we see only Tristan, motionless, asking himself dully: "The old tune, why does it wake me?" And what earlier seemed to us like a hollow sigh from the core of being now merely wants to say to us how "desolate and empty the sea." And where, breathless, we once thought we were being extinguished in a convulsive distention of all our feelings, and little remained to tie us to our present existence, we now hear and see only the hero wounded to death, yet not dying, with his despairing cry: "Longing! Longing! In death still longing! For very longing not dying!" (III 1: 132)

Thus in the enactment of the tragic myth the Dionysian is projected into Apollinian images. But, finally, the myth brings those images to a limit at which they are taken back again into the womb from which they have come. Then commences the "metaphysical swansong"—in the voice of Isolde, singing the *Liebestod:*

> In the rapture ocean's
> billowing roll,
> in the fragrance waves'
> ringing sound,
> in the world breath's
> wafting whole—
> to drown, to sink—
>   unconscious—highest joy!
>
> (III 1: 137)

Sliding more and more from its earlier "theoretical" stance, slipping toward the very discourse of the Wagnerian music dramas, reinscribing the lyric poetry that Wagner wrote for them, almost as if writing music, Nietzsche's text drifts finally into translating something of what that "theoretical" stance has produced into the tragic myth of *The Ring of the Nibelungen*. Recalling the image suggested earlier of Schopenhauer as Dürer's knight with death and devil, now envisioning such a knight sunk in slumber, Nietzsche writes:

From this abyss the Dionysian song rises to our ears to let us know that this German knight is still dreaming his primordial Dionysian myth in blissfully serious visions. Let no one believe that the German spirit has forever lost its mythical home when it can still understand so clearly the voices of the birds that tell of that home. Some day it will find itself awake in all the morning freshness following a monstrous sleep: then it will slay dragons, destroy vicious dwarves, wake Brünnhilde—and even Wotan's spear will not be able to obstruct its way. (III 1: 150)

And yet, *The Birth of Tragedy* returns finally to the Greeks. Setting the stage for the concluding invitation, for the old Athenian's invitation to follow him to a tragedy, the penultimate paragraph imagines a man's return to ancient Greek existence. The scene depicted could hardly be more different from that of the Wagnerian dragons, dwarves, and heroines:

Walking under lofty Ionic colonnades, looking up toward a horizon cut off by pure and noble lines, finding reflections of his transfigured shape in the shining marble at his side, and all around him solemnly striding or delicately moving men, with harmoniously sounding speech and a rhythmic language of gestures—in view of his continual influx of beauty, would he not have to exclaim, raising his hand to Apollo: "Blessed people of Hellas! How great must Dionysus be among you if the god of Delos considers such magic necessary to heal your dithyrambic madness! (III 1: 151–52)

It is as if another writing were almost ready to commence, even though it will not see the light of day until fourteen years later. It is as if Nietzsche were already beginning to trace, ever so lightly, the differentiation that will eventually—and emphatically—be marked between modern Germany and ancient Greece, the differentiation by which German music—to say nothing of the stories of the German spirit that Nietzsche will confess to having told on the basis of the latest German music—will come to be called "the most un-Greek of all possible art-forms" (III 1: 14). Thus a writing that will no longer reinscribe Wagnerian music. A writing that will serve to liberate another voice, one foreign to Wagnerian music, a strange voice.

"It should have sung . . ."

The inscription of a text such as Nietzsche's is necessarily topical. There belongs to it a certain placement, or, rather, a self-placement, in the sense that the text comes to be placed by virtue of—in and through—its very inscription. Both through what is said and through the way in which it is said, such a text places itself with respect to what is said. In the saying the text enacts a certain placement with regard to what is said, placing itself thus at some topos within whatever topical schema it outlines. Or, perhaps, setting itself adrift within the space thus outlined.

Furthermore, the inscription of a text such as Nietzsche's rarely fails to include moments at which the text turns thematically toward its own placement, engaging in a certain topology of inscription, inscribing its topology. Thus, at that juncture where *The Birth of Tragedy,* knocking at the gates of present and future, has just posed the question of the music-practicing Socrates, a topological reflection intervenes. Nietzsche writes: "Concerned but not hopeless, we stand aside a little while, contemplative men to whom it has been granted to be witnesses of these monstrous struggles and transitions" (III 1: 98). Thus, at this juncture, where the rigorously ordered analysis comes to something of a conclusion, Nietzsche's text is placed outside the opposition that has come to be posed between the tragic and the Socratic, placed in a certain proximity to Apollinian contemplation, that detached contemplation from a distance, almost as if in a dream. And yet, as soon as it is thus placed, there comes a gentle reminder that one can only defer, not escape, being engaged in the opposition, having the text placed within it: "Alas, it is the magic of these struggles that those who behold them must also fight in them." And, indeed, beyond this point the engagement of Nietzsche's text becomes unmistakable.

Yet, in a sense Nietzsche's text must have taken sides from the outset; for what it proposes is to make a contribution to aesthetic science. To this extent its discourse cannot but be theoretical, placing itself at a pole that would be difficult to differentiate from that of Socratism.

Nonetheless, the text slides again and again away from the theoretical pole. This displacement is most unmistakably indicated when, at the end of section 5, Nietzsche writes:

Thus all our knowledge of art is basically quite illusory, because as knowing beings we are not one and identical with that being that, as the sole creator and spectator of this comedy of art, prepares a perpetual entertainment for itself. Only insofar as the genius in the act of artistic creation coalesces with this primal artist of the world, does he know anything of the eternal essence of art. (III 1: 43–44)

This reflection serves notice that Nietzsche's text *as* a theoretical text crosses itself out, places itself under erasure, indeed placing under erasure the very placement with which it commenced. And yet, on the other hand, it goes ahead with its series of rigorously ordered analyses, goes ahead with making its contribution to aesthetic science; that is, the erasure, the displacement from the theoretical pole, remains largely unmarked, unreflected in the text, even though what comes to be said only furthers that displacement and renders the erasure more indispensable than ever. In other words, the text remains at variance with itself, remains divided from itself, lacking identity. One could describe it even as a text that exceeds itself by saying what it could not as such (as the theoretical text it purports to be) say; thus thematizing its proximity to the Dionysian, one would begin to sense the complexity of its inscription.

Two directions in which Nietzsche's text slides away from its initial theoretical topos are conspicuous. The first is defined by what is said in the text about the course through which the theoretical runs, the trajectory followed by Socratism—or, rather, about the outcome of its running that course, its self-destruction. For what is thus said cannot but undermine the very saying as simply a theoretical pronouncement—that is, it can be said only from out of that very self-destruction that it would announce, only through a certain reenactment of the self-destruction of Socratism that is said to have taken place in the work of Kant and—in a way more inclined toward renewing the need for art—in that of Schopenhauer. Here one can begin to see how the almost invisible erasure is operative in Nietzsche's text: in the reinscription of the text of Schopenhauer. For what is thus written into Nietzsche's text is not simply a metaphysics of the will, not simply a conceptual framework that one would like to eliminate from that text; rather, that reinscription serves precisely to mark the limit of theoretical knowledge by repeating within the text what was achieved by Schopenhauer, repeating it even more rigorously, letting the thing-in-itself slide toward the abyss, letting *Erscheinung* slide too (or rather explode) in a complex of movements, one of them toward *Schein*. By means of the reinscription within the text of *The Birth of Tragedy,* that text enacts—and so can announce—the self-suspension of Socratism at the edge of the abyss.

There is a second direction in which Nietzsche's text slides away from the theoretical pole, namely, toward art, toward tragedy, toward writing music. This direction is indicated even before the text commences: in the "Foreword to Richard Wagner," Nietzsche places his text within a certain circuit of exchange with Wagner the artist, whom he calls even his predecessor. And he declares already—before he begins—that "art represents the highest task and the genuinely metaphysical activity of this life." Yet it is especially in the final sections of *The Birth of Tragedy* that the shift in the direction of art comes openly into play: when Nietzsche's writing turns into interpretation of Wagner's music dramas, when it slips into the very discourse of the music dramas, almost as if writing music, when it comes to translate what has been said into the tragic myth of the Wagnerian heroes.

Later his writing turns again on itself. In 1886 Nietzsche wrote for the new edition of *The Birth of Tragedy* an "Attempt at a Self-Critique." Like other such texts (for example, the belated prefaces so entitled), this new foreword or afterward (both self-designations occur in the text) turns back upon the earlier text so as to outline the space of its reading and writing, thematizing the topology of the book's inscription. Of course, from that distance there are also various retractions, though even they are not without links to the topology of the text: the withdrawal of German music from "the grandiose *Greek problem*" (III 1: 14); and the withdrawal from Schopenhauer, Nietzsche's regret that he "tried laboriously to express by means of Schopenhauerian and Kantian formulas strange and new valuations that basically went against Kant's and Schopenhauer's spirit and taste!" (III 1: 13). Much the same withdrawal will be sounded two years later in *Ecce Homo,* which will declare of *The Birth of Tragedy* that "the cadaverous perfume of Schopenhauer sticks only to a few formulas" (VI 3: 308). But what is most striking to Nietzsche as he turns back to *The Birth of Tragedy* is the strangeness with which it had by that time come to appear. In the "Attempt at a Self-Critique" he calls it a "questionable book," "a strange and almost inaccessible book," "an impossible book" (III 1: 5, 7–8). He exclaims: "how strange [*fremd*] it appears now"—even though to one who "has not become a stranger to the task that this audacious book ventured for the first time" (III 1: 8). What, above all, makes the book questionable, almost inaccessible, impossible, is the strange voice, the foreign voice, that sounds from it:

What spoke here was a *strange* voice [*eine* fremde *Stimme*], the disciple of a still "unknown god," one who concealed himself for the time being under the scholar's hood. . . . What spoke here . . . was something like a mystical, almost maenadic soul that stammered with difficulty and voluntarily, as in a strange tongue, almost undecided whether it should communicate or conceal itself. (III 1: 8–9)

Whereas:

It should have *sung,* this "new soul"—and not spoken! What I had to say then—too bad that I did not dare say it as a poet: I could perhaps have done so! (III 1: 9)

But not—Nietzsche would now say, even at the risk of a certain retrospective appropriation—as a Wagnerian hero sings, nor as Isolde sings the *Liebestod.* Rather, a song to which one could dance, a song of holy laughter.

Index

INDEX

Mask, 43, 43 n. 1, 89, 115, 121
Menander, 111
Midas (King), 36
Mimesis: art as, 20–21; and learning, 27; and original, 30; and Apollinian, 33, 89, 97–98; and nature, 68–69; Dionysian, 71, 89–90; Dionysian and Apollinian, 84, 87–88; and images, 85; directionality of, 86; and music, 86; double, 88, 90–91; and chorus, 89; Socratic and tragic, 137
Monster(s), 5, 14, 18
Monstrosity: as Dionysian, 78, 92, 129; and Oedipus, 89; and Empedocles, 108; and Euripides, 117; Socrates as, 124
Monstrous: desert, 3; opposition, 20; defect, 125; difference, 141; symphonic movement, 143; struggles, 147
Moral concepts, 127
Mothers of being, 96, 109
Music: and Socrates, 4, 131; and sculpture, 17; Dionysian, 19 n. 5, 90; and Apollo, 23n; birthplace of 54 n. 10; and art, 56, 83, 94; and the primal one, 69; Dionysian and Apollinian, 72, 72 n. 22; and will, 73, 83; and nature, 73; Wagnerian, 73 n. 23; Greek, 73, 73 n. 23, 139; saving deed of, 74; and life, 75; as voice, 75 n. 25; and mimesis, 75 n. 25; and sublime, 84, 137, 141; and ecstasy, 87; discourse on, 87; and tragedy, 88, 96; and image, 97; and myth, 99–100; and spirit, 103, 132; and philosophy, 103; and chorus, 121, 121 n. 8; cosmic, 124; German, 136, 138, 139, 141–45, 149; and thought, 139 n. 32; and Wagner, 140; and abyss, 142; writing, 131, 144, 149
Music drama, 111 n. 1, 125 n. 11, 142–44, 149
Mystic, 125, 134 n. 22, 150

Myth: and opposition, 57 n. 12; and tragedy, 99, 143, 144, 149; and character, 111 n. 1; and *Republic*, 128; and logic, 134 n. 22; and history, 135 n. 23; Dionysian, 144
Mythology, 36 n. 27

Nature: and art, 20–21, 25, 33; and the Apollinian, 21; and will, 66; mimetic double of, 92; inversions of, 124
New Attic Comedy, 109, 111
Nonwriter, 126, 130–31
Novel, 127

Oedipus: as hero, 42; and wretchedness, 76, 83; and Dionysus, 89; wonderful end of, 100; and Socrates, 129–30
Oedipus at Colonus, 36 n. 26, 79, 80, 82
Oedipus Rex, 54 n. 10
Oedipus Tyrannos: and draft, 6; and *Geschlecht,* 31; and Dionysus, 43; and *The Bacchae,* 47 n. 6; and nature, 73 n. 24; and σωφροσύνη 79; and separation, 80
"On Reading and Writing," 9
"On Truth and Lies in a Nonmoral Sense," 7, 87 n. 5
Opposites, 100, 105–6, 110
Opposition: Apollinian and Dionysian, 14, 20, 23n, 55, 56, 57 n. 12, 99 n. 13, 137; and art, 15–18; monstrous, 17, 18, 56, 83; and tragedy, 19, 109, 147; Apollinian/Platonism, 31; and appearances, 66, 67, 135; and plurality, 70; spectators and chorus, 90; sublime and beautiful, 95; suffering and joy, 100; and space, 100; Dionysian and Socratic, 121, 129–30; intuition and concept, 128; and Socratic, 131, 137, 147

155